FOR THE
LOVE OF THE
HORSE

—— Looking Back, Looking Forward ——

Mark Rashid

Foreword by Dr. Steve Peters, MS, PsyD, ABPN

TRAFALGAR SQUARE
North Pomfret, Vermont

First published in 2022 by
Trafalgar Square Books
North Pomfret, Vermont 05053

Disclaimer of Liability
The author and publisher shall have neither liability nor responsibility to any person or entity with
respect to any loss or damage caused or alleged to be caused directly or indirectly by the information
contained in this book. While the book is as accurate as the author can make it, there may be errors,
omissions, and inaccuracies.

Some names and identifying details have been changed to protect the privacy of individuals.

Library of Congress Cataloging-in-Publication Data
Names: Rashid, Mark, author. | Peters, Steve (Sports psychiatrist), writer of foreword.
Title: For the love of the horse : looking back, looking forward / Mark Rashid;
foreword by Steve Peters, MS, PsyD, ABPN.
Description: North Pomfret, Vermont : Trafalgar Square Books, 2022.
Summary: "Renowned horseman and popular storyteller Mark Rashid looks
back on his evolution since the publication of his first book
Considering the Horse over 20 years ago. He ponders the transformative
moments and impactful individuals who have helped shape his philosophy
of horse training and care. In his familiar way, he shares lessons he
has learned through stories of his own horses and those he's met, and
considers how far horsemanship has come and how bright its future might be"
—Provided by publisher.

Identifiers: LCCN 2022011140 | ISBN 9781646011391 (paperback)
ISBN 9781646011407 (epub)
Subjects: LCSH: Horses--Training. | Horses--Behavior.
Horsemanship--Anecdotes. | Horse trainers--Anecdotes.
Classification: LCC SF287 .R263 2022 | DDC 636.1/0835--dc23/eng/20220411
LC record available at https://lccn.loc.gov/2022011140

Book design by HighTide Design
Cover design by RM Didier
Typefaces Horley Old Style MT
Printed in the United States of America
10 9 8 7 6 5 4 3 2 1

CONTENTS

Foreword

Mark Rashid begins *For the Love of the Horse* by revisiting his first book, *Considering the Horse: Tales of Problems Solved and Lessons Learned*. He recounts how his first book was in danger of not getting published and how he had to hold his ground to keep the title.

Considering the Horse: Tales of Problems Solved and Lessons Learned" could easily have been an appropriate title for this book, too. In it, he shares with us the accumulation of nearly a half-century of solving problems and learning lessons.

He also states that when writing his first book, he did not want it to be a "how-to" book. Well, if you are observant, you will realize that is exactly what *For the Love of the Horse* is. It's not a book of step-by-step instruction but of lessons to guide you and to reflect on in your own journey with horses.

The lessons found in these pages reflect who Mark is and how he leads his life. Following Mark on this journey of several decades with horses, you will see how the principles of the martial art *aikido* and its adaptation for horse people, *aibado*, nurture an inner stillness and softness that has informed his work with horses and teaching.

In reading Mark's words, you realize that he has been able to maintain the "beginner's open and questioning mind," which is very difficult to do when you have become as accomplished as he has.

In these pages, once again Mark's boyhood mentor, Walter ("the old man") shows up in ways you might not expect. If ever a statement epitomized empathy and humanity in interacting with horses, it's Walter's comment: "How do you think the horse feels about all this?" This same theme of kindness, calm, and quiet when dealing with horses is felt throughout the book.

I have thoroughly enjoyed the discussions I've had with Mark and have been impressed with his insatiable thirst for knowledge. He is everything you would expect of a good scientist. As you read this book, you will become familiar with how he is always questioning, observing, and learning while remaining humble without ego. He wants to know more for the horse, himself, and his students and readers. I know first-hand that just as remarkable is his ability to understand neurological concepts, articulate them, and most importantly, apply them in a way that is in tune with the horse's nervous system.

I believe this is the most important book that Mark has written thus far. It is well worth reading these pages, as there are enlightening and profound lessons throughout. After all, what would you expect from a great "how-to" book?

Dr. Steve Peters, MS, PsyD, ABPN
Co Author of *Evidence-Based Horsemanship* with Martin Black

Preface

A while ago I needed to get something out of our downstairs storage room. On the wall that separates the storage room from our guest room hangs a nicely framed display of my first two books, *Considering the Horse: Tales of Problems Solved and Lessons Learned*, and *A Good Horse Is Never a Bad Color*. I can't even begin to guess how many times I've walked past that frame over the years, but I do know it's been enough to where I seldom, if ever, even look at it anymore. On this particular day in the spring of 2021, however, I felt the need to stop and take a look.

A few things passed through my mind as I stood there. The first was how well the workmanship of the framing itself has held up over the years. It was done by a friend who owned a frame shop here in town back in the day, and it took him nearly a month to complete. Then it dawned on me that both he and his frame shop have been gone now for over twenty years.

The realization that my friend has been gone that long caused me to also realize that *Considering the Horse*, my very first book, must also be over twenty years old. But how could that be? It seems like I wrote it only a few short months ago. Looking at *Considering the Horse* in the frame, I found myself doing the math:

We had commissioned the frame right after *A Good Horse...* was released, and my friend passed in 1997. That meant the frame was most likely done in 1996.

Considering the Horse was released two or three years before *A Good Horse...*, which would put its release date in 1993.

Really? I went upstairs to the bookshelf in our office where Crissi keeps the books we both have written and checked the publication date inside the copy of *Considering the Horse*. Sure enough, it was released in 1993. That meant *Considering the Horse* would soon be turning 30-years old!

I started thinking about how dramatically the trajectory of my life changed with the publication of that little book and over the next few weeks began wondering about possible ways to commemorate its upcoming anniversary. Initially, writing another book didn't really enter the equation. I have all but shifted away from writing books in recent years and turned my energy to writing movie scripts, one of which recently picked up a little traction and moved into the development stage.

Yet the more I thought about it, the more I started to lean toward the possibility of an anniversary book (for lack of a better term). Two big questions loomed. The first was: did I even have anything to say that would be worthwhile to a reader? The second was: if I did have something worthwhile to say, would it be enough to fill an entire book?

Not long after that, I began jotting down a few ideas about things I thought folks might find interesting. Those ideas eventually turned into an outline, and the outline eventually turned into the book you now hold.

Included in this book are many important concepts, principles, and even science-based information that has had a huge impact on my work with horses (and people). Much of this I find very exciting, and I hope you will find it equally exciting and helpful in your own horsemanship journey.

Also included in this book are a few stories that folks who have spent time with some of my books in the past might find a bit familiar. That is by design. There are certain experiences in all our lives that we can look back on, and with hindsight, understand how those moments have become important touchstones or turning points that shaped who we are today.

While I don't believe living in the past is ever a good thing, I do believe revisiting those important life moments on occasion can be a healthy reminder of not only where we've been, but where we're going. It also gives us an opportunity to hopefully experience those past moments from a new perspective of growth and learning.

After all, what would an anniversary book be if we didn't reminisce at least a little.

Thank you for picking up *For the Love of the Horse*, and I wish you all peace, health and happiness.

Mark Rashid

Estes Park, Colorado

CHAPTER 1

The Book That Almost Wasn't

"When you get to the fork in the road, take it."
YOGI BERRA

I was between ranching jobs in the summer of 1991 when I came up with the idea of starting a small horse training school as a way to help pay the bills. It wasn't anything elaborate, just five or six students, most with limited horse experience and all just looking for ways to get better.

The horses we used came from the BLM (Bureau of Land Management) Mustang program. These were horses recently gathered in Nevada and shipped to the Cañon City Prison in Colorado where inmates would be taught to handle and train them. I'd met the man in charge of the program during a chance encounter a year or so earlier. It was at a small horse expo in Denver where I was asked to do a demonstration with Mustangs provided by the BLM. He gave me his card after the demo, and I used it to call and ask if I could get the loan of a couple of horses to use for my fledgling school. He was happy to oblige.

About two months into the program, one of the students, a woman named Julie, came up to me after class and mentioned that her husband was thinking about selling his horse. She asked if I could come and have a look at the gelding and let them know how much I thought he'd be worth. I told her I could stop by that evening and that's how I ended up standing in their corral, halter and rope in the crook of my arm, watching the big palomino charge nervously around the inside of the pen.

"Like I said," Julie's husband Scott remarked as the couple stood just outside the corral fence. "He can be a little tough to catch."

The horse, whose name was Max, darted around the few ponderosa pines that grew in the pen, stampeded behind the three-sided shelter inside of which a chestnut mare stood lazily swishing flies with her tail, emerged from behind the shelter and went bucking and farting to the opposite end of the enclosure. Before I could do or say anything, and without a bit of hesitation on his part, he wheeled and repeated the exact same path he just took using the same speed and intensity.

I stood and watched Max career around in this pattern for a few minutes before stepping out in front of him as he came near, causing him to slide to a stop, turn, and take off in the opposite direction, repeating the same pattern in reverse. After a couple laps in that direction, I stepped in front of him again. He jammed on the brakes, turned, and went back to the original direction for a couple laps before I stepped in front of him again. This went on for a few minutes longer before he finally just stopped and let me approach.

As it turned out, catching wasn't the only thing Max was struggling with. Once he was caught, he didn't want to be haltered. Once haltered, he didn't want to follow. Once he was following, we found he didn't understand boundaries and would run into the person in front of him. Once that was taken care of, he didn't want to stand to be saddled. Once he was saddled, he wouldn't let you get on. Once you were on, he wouldn't go. Once he would go, he wouldn't stop.

In almost every case where he exhibited unwanted behavior, it seemed all we needed to do was be clear about what we really wanted from him. Doing so created a positive change in him usually within just a matter of minutes. To that end, it became clear almost from the start this was a willing horse that simply became confused about what was expected of him. Once we cleared up the misunderstandings,

Max not only became much calmer, but quite amenable to most any request as well.

A couple hours later and having seen just how nice his horse really was, Scott decided he wasn't going to sell him after all. Instead, he wanted to keep him and see if he could get things worked out a little better between the two of them.

Julie and Scott followed me to my truck as I was getting ready to leave. "Have you ever thought about writing a book about how you work with horses?" Scott asked, seemingly out of the blue.

I'd only known Scott for a couple hours, but during that time picked up on the fact that he had a somewhat dry sense of humor. So, when he asked the question, I just assumed he was kidding. I instinctively let out a little chuckle, both at what I perceived as him making a joke as well as the idea that anyone might be even remotely interested in reading a whole book about how I worked with horses.

Unlike other times when he cracked a joke, however, this time he didn't follow it up with the hint of a smile. My chuckle subsided as I began to realize he might be serious.

"A book?"

"I read the articles you wrote for *Western Horseman*," he said. "I liked them."

Ah, the *Western Horseman* articles.

A couple years earlier while working as the livery manager at one of the local guest ranches, I hired a fellow by the name of Matt Bowers to help out for the fall and winter season. As it turned out, Matt was a fairly well-connected marketing director who was between marketing jobs and looking for some temporary work with horses.

It was Matt's idea, after watching me work through a problem with a troubled horse, to submit an article to *Western Horseman* magazine about what I'd done to help the horse. It turned out Matt knew the senior editor at the magazine and after a phone introduction and explanation of what I'd done with the horse, the editor agreed to take a look at an article. So, I wrote and submitted it. Not only did that article get published in the magazine, but the editor then gave me a list of several other subjects to write about, all of which also made it into the magazine.

"I've never thought about writing a book," I told Scott.

"You should," he replied. "And if you do, I can help."

It turned out Scott owned his own publishing house, which operated in part under a bigger publishing company. The company was based literally just down the road in Boulder and up till then focused primarily on historical books about the West. The folks there were looking for titles to help them break into the horse book market, and Scott thought a book from me might be just what they were looking for.

"Thanks," I said as we shook hands and I climbed in my truck. "I'll definitely keep that in mind."

And that was that. Almost as soon as I pulled out of the driveway the idea of writing a book completely left my consciousness. To be honest, I had more pressing matters on my mind, such as how I was going to make a steady living once summer ended and my four-month horse training school was over. Sure, I almost always had private clients who were looking for lessons or training. But the work was sporadic at best and got increasingly more so once the cold weather set in.

Not that it mattered much anyway, seeing as how back then I gave away almost as much of my time to clients as I charged them for. It was a practice I felt only fair as I was often working through my own (sometimes steep) learning curves when it came to training and teaching. Still, the practice of giving time away wasn't terribly helpful financially, especially with a wife, three small children, and plenty of bills to pay.

Then, one evening about two weeks after having met Scott and spending time with his horse, the phone rang. This was still at a time when phones hung on the wall, and you physically answered it to find out who was on the other end. Cell phones were still in their infancy and for the most part lived in black bags that weighed as much as a small child, took up so much space that if one was on the bench seat of your pickup you couldn't have a passenger, and could only get service on Tuesday afternoon and Thursday morning, so long as the weather was good and there wasn't a tree, park bench, or dog anywhere nearby to interfere with the signal.

"Hello?"

"Is this Mark? The voice on the other end of the line asked.

'Yes."

"This is Scott, you worked with my horse, Max, a couple weeks ago."

"Oh, yeah. Hi, Scott. Everything okay?"

"Everything's good," he said, a smile in his voice. "Max and I are getting along great."

"Good. I'm glad to hear…"

"The reason I'm calling," he interrupted, "is to see if you've given any more thought to writing that book."

"Book?"

"Yeah, the one we talked about when you were over here."

"Um…No, I haven't given…"

"I have a meeting with the publisher in Boulder tomorrow, so if you have an outline ready, I'd take it down and pitch it to them."

I didn't have an outline. In fact, I didn't even know what an outline was, much less how to put one together. And besides, I wasn't a writer. Certainly not in the technical sense, or any other sense for that matter. Why was this guy trying to talk me into being one? I had no business trying to write a book. I was a horse guy. People who write books are smart and articulate and usually have something clever to say. I didn't have any of those qualities.

At least that's what the mental gymnastics in my head churned out in the moments between what he just said and what I was about to say.

"I'm not a writer."

"Yes, you are. I've read your articles."

"Writing an article is one thing. Writing a book is completely different." I said this with all the authority of someone who knew very little about either.

"Writing is writing," came his reply.

"But…"

"How about this. What are the qualities of a horse book you'd want to read?"

I had to stop and think. I hadn't actually read that many horse books lately, and lost interest pretty quickly in the ones I did try to read because they were of the how-to, textbook-type variety, for which I never developed a liking.

"Not a how-to book," I said. "I like books that tell a story. Like the kind James Herriot wrote."

"Okay," Scott said. "What about artwork inside the book? Yes or no?"

"I always liked the illustrations in Will James' books."

For those who may not know, James Herriot was an English veterinarian who wrote a series of anecdotal books chronicling his practice from the 1930s to the 1950s. He was one of my favorite authors. Will James was a cowboy, writer, and artist who did most of his writing in the 1920s and 30s. He also did his own illustrations. One of his best books, in my opinion, was *Smokey the Cowhorse*.

"What about subject matter?" Scott asked.

"Pretty much anything I'm interested in."

"What about problem-solving?"

"Yeah, I suppose."

"I think the horse world needs a problem-solving book." the smile was back in his voice. "I had no idea Max misunderstood what I wanted. I thought he hated me. I bet there's a lot more people out there that feel the same way about their horses and for the same reasons."

"Maybe so." I found myself nodding in agreement.

I didn't have any real way of knowing at the time, but the conversation I was about to follow would ultimately have a most profound impact on my life, and my future. But then, that's just the way things go sometimes.

———————

Over the next two hours, Scott and I worked out the framework for what would ultimately become my first book, *Considering the Horse: Tales of Problems Solved and Lessons Learned*, although getting to the title would be a whole other process that wouldn't come until much later.

By the time we finished our conversation that night, Scott had the entire outline he needed and the next day he went in and pitched the idea to the publisher. He called me the following evening to let me know they were interested, but before they would commit, they would first need to see at least two full chapters.

It was about then that, for me, the reality of the situation began to set in. I admittedly got caught up in Scott's enthusiasm during our conversation the night before and pretty much talked myself into the idea that, yeah, I could definitely write a book. Heck, why not? In fact, the longer we talked, the more excited about the idea I got. Of course, it's always easy to get excited about an *idea* when there's no actual skin in the game.

But now with the news that an actual publisher was actually interested in me writing an actual book, things seemed to get very real very quickly.

I didn't get much sleep that night. I tossed and turned, worrying whether I had what it took to write this thing. I got up and walked around, opened the refrigerator and looked inside, walked around some more, opened the refrigerator again, sat on the couch, stared out the window, paced the hallway, looked in the refrigerator.

And then, sometime between midnight and around three in the morning, something dawned on me. Ever since I was little, I have always believed I could do anything I set my mind to, from teaching myself how to play drums and guitar, to skydiving, building my own stringed instruments, retracing the Lewis and Clark Expedition on the Missouri River in a canoe, becoming a martial artist, learning to be an equine bodyworker, and even becoming a sound engineer.

As I stood looking in the refrigerator for what was probably was the seventeenth time that night, it finally became clear that if this book was going to be written, all I needed to do was decide I was going to do it and then that would be that.

The next morning, I began writing. And when I say I was writing, that is exactly what I was doing. Writing—the old-fashioned way, with an ink pen and on a yellow legal pad. Having absolutely no use for the minimal typing skills I developed while taking an elective typing class in high school to get a cheap credit, I decided it would be easier and faster for me to write everything out in longhand than it would be to try to type.

In this way I finished the first chapter in a little over a week. The second chapter was finished in one week more. Then for good measure, I wrote a third chapter. From those handwritten pages, my wife (who unlike me, was a proficient typist) typed everything into a secondhand word processor we picked up somewhere, and when she was finished, I gave the chapters to Scott, and he in turn gave them to the publisher.

In the meantime, and at Scott's suggestion, I spoke with my friend, Ron Ball, a Western artist whose artwork strongly resembled that of Will James. Ron happily agreed to do the artwork for the inside of the book, as well as the cover, should the publisher decide to do it.

Another month would pass before we heard anything from the publisher, and when we did it was because they wanted to schedule a meeting with Scott and me at their corporate office in Boulder.

On the day I arrived for the meeting, a very pleasant woman named Mira met me in the lobby and proceeded to give me a tour of the entire operation, including the shop where they printed the books. After that she took me into a little meeting room where Scott, a woman named Barbara, who turned out to be the owner of the company, and Steve, the marketing director, were already waiting.

After introductions and a few minutes of small talk, the purpose of the meeting finally came to light.

"We really like what you've written." Barbara smiled. "And we'd like to offer you a contract on your book."

It struck me as strange that she used the words *your book*. Up until that very moment I hadn't thought of it as *my* book. In my mind it was *the* book or *a* book, but not *my* book.

She opened a manila folder sitting on the table in front of her and took out some papers.

"We've taken the liberty of drawing up a contract." She handed the pages to me. "You'll see it's pretty standard. And if you're okay with signing today, we can cut your advance check before you leave."

"Advance check?" I questioned. Scott and I had numerous conversations since this whole thing began, but in none of them did we talk about how I would be paid. It's almost embarrassing to admit that at the time I knew absolutely nothing about payment practices in the book industry and what an advance was or how it worked.

"Yes," Barbara said. "It's in the contract, there. We'll give you half of your advance today, the other half when the completed manuscript is delivered."

"Advance?" I repeated. The room fell silent for a couple of seconds while it registered with everybody I had no idea what she was talking about.

"Against your future royalties," Scott chimed in. "It's to help you out financially while you write the book. All authors get them. Once the book is out and starts to sell, your advance will automatically be deducted from your royalties until it's paid back. From then on, the rest of the royalties go in your pocket."

"Oh. Yeah. Okay."

Scott, who ended up being my editor for the project, was kind enough to walk me through the contract and explain it in terms so that a horse guy could understand. Looking back, I probably should have consulted an attorney, but at the time I wouldn't have been able to afford one anyway. So, I took Scott's word, signed the contract, and walked out with a check worth more money than I'd seen in quite a while.

Surprisingly, especially after all the initial self-doubt and worry about the whole thing, I found that the actual process of writing the book relatively easy. Once I decided on a basic premise for the content, which ended up being a combination of stories about Walter, the old horseman I'd worked for when I was a kid, and stories of things I'd been doing with horses since then, I was able to get into a comfortable rhythm that lasted until the book was finished.

That doesn't necessarily mean everything about the process for the book was comfortable, however. For example, trying to figure out a title took a little doing. We did have a working title for the initial submission, but I don't recall what it was, and we got rid of it pretty much as soon as I signed the contract anyway.

I was four or five chapters into writing the book when Scott suggested we start getting serious about figuring out what we were going to call the thing. To that end, both Scott and I wrote down as many potential titles as we could think of, then one by one we started eliminating the ones we couldn't agree on or that we didn't like.

After a week or two, we finally whittled the list down to two prospective titles, one that Scott came up with and one that I came up with. "Considering the Horse" was mine and Scott's was "Through the Eyes of Horses." We sent both titles to the publisher to get their feedback, and the preference they gave (given the content of the pages they'd seen so far) was for "Considering the Horse." The caveat was they wanted to eliminate the "ing" from the word "Considering," making the title "Consider the Horse."

I didn't like the change. Using the word "Consider" felt like a demand, as if we were telling readers what they should do. That was not at all the feel or intention I wanted the book to represent. The whole idea from the start was to show we were making an effort to be considerate of horses when we worked with them, to offer real-life stories about situations—good, bad, and indifferent—and then allow readers to decide whether the information was useful to them or not. I felt very strongly that the title should embody the idea of choice. To that end, in my view the word "Consider*ing*" represented something ongoing and active, a decision we were making and with which we were ultimately attempting to follow through.

A number of discussions took place during the next several weeks regarding those three letters. But in the end, and with Scott's enthusiastic recommendation based on the chapters I was sending him, the publisher finally agreed to the word "Considering."

By this time, we were well into winter, and I was about halfway through writing the book when I received a call from Steve, the marketing guy at the publishing company. With little more than a cordial "Hi, how are you?" he turned immediately to the purpose of his call.

"I've been doing some research into horse books," he said, a matter-of-fact tone to his voice. "I've bought and read the current top five horse books on the market."

"Okay…?" My response was more of a question than a statement.

"I've also read everything you've submitted so far."

"Okay…?" I repeated.

"Every one of these top-selling books are how-to books."

"Uh-huh."

"What you're writing is not a how-to book," he said it as if it were a surprise.

"No, it's not," I agreed.

"Why isn't it?"

"I'm not sure I understand the question."

"Why is your book not a how-to book?"

There was a long confusion-induced silence on my part.

During the meeting in which I signed the contract (and at which Steve was present) we discussed at some length the anecdotal nature of book. In fact, the storytelling was one of the main selling points, and according to Barbara, the owner, a big reason why they wanted to publish it in the first place. To suddenly be asked why the book wasn't something that it was never supposed to be, especially four months and six chapters into it, was a little disconcerting.

As the conversation progressed, the reasons for Steve's concern over what we now agreed would publish as *Considering the Horse* became ever more apparent. First, and as he already stated, all the top-selling horse training books at the time were of the step-by-step, how-to nature. For that reason, he'd come to the conclusion readers of horse training books preferred that type of book.

I suggested perhaps the reason how-to books seemed so popular was because they were more or less the only option available at the time. I supposed given a choice, horse folks might gravitate to something a little less rigid. He didn't buy it.

The second, and probably most important reason Steve was so concerned about *Considering the Horse* was he wasn't clear on how to market it.

"Is this a story book?" he asked. "Or is it a training book?"

"A little of both," I replied.

"It really should be one or the other," he insisted, "especially from a marketing standpoint."

To be fair, the publisher only had one other horse title at the time, a book on pack horses, and it'd been in publication long before Steve became the marketing director. As a result, he didn't have any experience whatsoever promoting any kind of horse book, much less one that, in his view, didn't fit into a specific category.

Another factor here, and one I'm sure was playing heavily on Steve's mind, was the fact that the publisher was small and therefore quite financially conservative. According to Scott, they only took on titles they were ninety-nine percent sure would generate a return. The longer Steve and I spoke, the more I got the impression he didn't think *Considering the Horse* would sell, and to that end, he didn't want to be held responsible for what he saw as the only book in the company's history to lose money.

Our conversation lasted perhaps 20 minutes and nothing I said during that time seemed to have any effect on how Steve was feeling about the situation. At the end of the call, just before hanging up, Steve told me in no uncertain terms he would be suggesting to the powers that be that my contract be voided, I pay back the advance, and we all go our separate ways.

I panicked. The advance was long gone, used to buy clothes for the kids, pay bills and buy food. It was wintertime and I didn't have a lot of horse work. I couldn't pay back the advance even if I wanted to.

I called Scott as soon as I hung up with Steve.

"Yeah," Scott said after hearing what happened. "He called me too. Let's not worry about it too much."

"But I can't pay back the advance."

"I don't think it'll come to that," he predicted. "Here's what we'll do. I'll stall 'em and you keep writing."

There was just the hint of a lilt in his voice that briefly reminded me of one of those old 1930s gangster movies. *"Yeah, Bugsy. Here's the plan, see? I'll stall 'em, and you make a run for it."*

After ridding myself of the image of Scott in a pin-striped suit and tie with a fedora tipped slightly to one side and a cigarette dangling precariously out from under a pencil-thin moustache, I suggested perhaps we might need a slightly better plan.

It was then he explained why he didn't think we needed to worry too much about the situation. As it turned out, the publisher had a certain production schedule for the new books they produced every year, and the schedule was usually in place a year or sometimes two ahead of time.

In a nutshell, the timetable hinged on when each individual book would physically to go into print, and that hinged on when each author submitted a completed manuscript. The way Scott described it, when the manuscript is in on time, the printing can begin on time. In other words, all authors were in their own production slot during the year. The further out from an author's deadline, the easier it would be for the publisher to replace them in the schedule if the need arose. The closer to the deadline, the more difficult it would be to find a replacement author to fit into that time slot.

We were still several months from when my book was due, but I was already about halfway finished and averaging a chapter every few weeks. At that rate I would be finished at least two months ahead of my deadline, maybe sooner. Scott figured if push came to shove and Steve was successful in getting the publisher to consider replacing me, all Scott would need to do was stall the publisher from making a decision for a month or so. If he could do that, there wouldn't be another author ready to fit into my slot in the production schedule and, in a sense, we would get published by default.

As it turned out, that was exactly what happened. Steve apparently argued his position effectively enough so the publisher began to have some serious doubts about my book. Soon after, Scott received a call from them in which they questioned the viability of *Considering the Horse* and were apparently giving some thought to

voiding my contract. True to his word, Scott was somehow able to stall their decision just long enough so they couldn't find another author. As a result, and as Scott
predicted, *Considering the Horse* was published by default.

⌒

Just because the book was on its way to being published didn't mean Steve changed
his view of it. The only promotion it received was an appearance in the publisher's
catalog prior to its release. In fact, even I became convinced my book wouldn't sell,
so much so that I just assumed it would be the only book I'd ever get the opportunity
to write. Because of that, at the last minute I added nearly an entire page of "thank
yous" to everybody I could think of who had helped me along my horsemanship
journey to that point.

Not surprisingly, once released, the book suffered dismal sales and, for a time,
it appeared that Steve was going to be right about it being a disaster for the company. But then something quite interesting happened. The book was sent out to a few
prominent horse publications in hopes of getting it reviewed, and a couple months
later, those reviews began coming in. The very first review the book received came
from *EQUUS* magazine. Among other things, it said, "...a Colorado clone of James
Herriot reveals the evolution of his training through well-told tales." The next review
came from the prestigious *Quarter Horse Journal*, "Rashid writes in an anecdotal
format about the universal truth that you don't come out a winner when you get your
results by force." That was followed by the equally prestigious *Paint Horse Journal*,
"Of literally hundreds of books on various aspects of horse care and horsemanship...
without a doubt...this is the most interesting."

Just like that, the book took off. The first printing sold out in just a few weeks. The
second, much larger printing sold out in a couple months. The third printing sold out
in a few months more. By the end of the year the publisher had gone through four
printings and was on its fifth. To date, *Considering the Horse* has been translated into
twelve different languages and has sold over a million copies worldwide.

⌒

As I mentioned earlier, I wrote the entire book on a yellow legal pad that my wife typed into a word processor and stored onto a floppy disc. For those of you who may not know, a floppy disc is what home computer pioneers used to use to store information. A floppy disc weighed forty pounds, was the size of dining room chair, and you could store about 1700 words on it, depending on font size.

At any rate, once I filled a disc with text, I would hand-deliver it to Scott, who would put it into his tiny-screened, room-sized computer, and together we would go over what I'd written.

"You know," I remember him saying on one of those final visits as we were closing in on the end of the writing and editing process. "This book is going to change things for people and their horses." He paused. "It's going to change things for you, too."

My primary concern at the time was just to get the book finished and off to the publisher before it could be pulled from the schedule, and I'd be forced to pay back the advance. The thought that it might change anything for anybody, especially me, never even made it to my radar.

Because of that, I had no way of knowing at the time just how prophetic Scott's words would become.

AN INTRODUCTION TO THE PAST

CHAPTER 2

Planted Seeds

*"Better than a thousand days of diligent
study is one day with a great teacher."*

JAPANESE PROVERB

Within the first few paragraphs of Considering the Horse, readers are introduced to Walter, the old horseman I began learning from when I was quite young. Walter was generally a man of few words. When he did speak, especially when it came to issues with horses, he usually used his words as a catalyst to inspire thought rather than to give instruction.

In the opening pages of *Considering the Horse* I shared a story in which he and I traveled to a neighboring ranch to pick up a load of hay. While there, we stopped to watch a few cowboys who were "breaking" a young mare in a round pen. The mare was snubbed to a post with a rag over her eyes while a saddle was strapped to her back.

I explained in the story how I found the rodeo that followed, once the rider was on her back and the mare turned loose, quite exciting. Not having ever seen anything like it before, nor having any real experience with horses other than what I'd seen in the B Western movies of the time, I just assumed what I was seeing was how working with horses was done.

That was until Walter, who was sitting next to me on the old, weathered round pen fence, posed a simple question in the middle of all the commotion: "How do you suppose the horse feels about all this?"

It was an incident that took place more than fifty years ago, and I can't begin to tell you how many times that question has popped into my head since. It's as if it lives somewhere deep in my subconscious, quietly lying in wait, suddenly making an appearance anytime I find myself producing or adding undue stress to a horse. It's become a familiar safety valve that, over time, has allowed me figure out how to head off potentially unfortunate situations before they actually become one.

Don't get me wrong. I've been in plenty of situations over the years where his question showed up while I was working with a troubled horse, only to have me completely override it. More times than not, my ill-advised choice always caused the situation to become way messier than it needed to be, and I would always kick myself for it later.

While those times have now become further and fewer between, especially in more recent years, the reasons for which we'll talk about later, it doesn't mean that I don't continue to rely on those subconscious-hidden words of his in all kinds of situations.

Truth be known, I believe much of what I picked up from Walter during our time together lay dormant in my subconscious until I began writing *Considering the Horse*. It was amazing, and actually quite comforting in a way, just how many memories of our time together came flooding back once I began writing. One memory would lead to another, then to another, and still another.

That being said, not all of those subconscious memories were as helpful as others.

Back in the late 1990s after I left ranching to pursue teaching clinics on the road, a guy by the name of Tim Hayes showed up at one of the very first clinics I was asked to do. The clinic was held in April at a venue just outside of Los Angeles, California, and Tim, who lived in New York, somehow heard about the clinic and flew out to participate. He borrowed a horse to ride and during the next four days, Tim and I became friends.

We kept in touch after that and a few weeks before Christmas that same year, Tim called and asked if he could come out to our place in Colorado between

Christmas and New Year's to hang out for a few days, talk horses, and maybe help out where needed. I told him there wouldn't be much going on horse-wise due to the unpredictable weather that time of year, along with the fact most of our horses would be out on winter pasture, but he was certainly welcome to come and hang out.

Now before going any further, I'd like to mention that in the same story I shared in *Considering the Horse* in which I recounted the incident about the young mare, I also mentioned a little quirk, if you will, that Walter had when it came to hauling hay. In particular, we would stack so much hay in the bed of his 1949 Ford pickup that it looked like a monkey sitting on a football. Then he would refuse to tie the load down, always proclaiming that we didn't have that far to go. Of course, as soon as we took the first turn out of the driveway where we'd picked up the hay, we'd lose the entire load and have to spend the next hour or so restacking the bales in the bed of the truck.

As it turned out, during Tim's visit I needed to pick up a load of hay from our hay supplier. We didn't need much, just twenty-three bales. So, with Tim riding shotgun, we drove the thirty-five miles down the mountain to our supplier's place in the "valley" and loaded the hay. There was nothing unusual about the stack itself. In fact, he and I stacked the load exactly as I did hundreds of times before. Ten bales on the bottom row, all facing north and south. Eight bales on the second row (four on the left side of the truck, four on the right) all facing east and west, and four bales, two by two, on the top row facing north and south.

This is a very stable way to stack hay as the bales are in a sense "tied" together due to the nature of the stack itself. Because of that, and the fact that it is not a tall stack to begin with, not even going above the cab of the truck, the chances of losing any bales going down the road without physically tying them together are pretty slim.

"You want to tie these down?" Tim asked as we put the last bale on the truck.

"Naw," I said. "We should be fine. Besides, we aren't going that far."

As we drove away from our hay supplier's place, a little breeze began to pick up.

We live on what is known as the eastern slope of the Rocky Mountains. Generally speaking, the way the winter weather works here is most of the snow and harsh cold will get dumped on the other side of the Continental Divide, over on the western slope. The Divide then acts a bit like a dam, stopping the snow from reaching us, while at the same time forcing pressure over the top of the mountains. This pressure often turns into fairly strong winds on our side of the Divide that can easily reach thirty to sixty miles per hour for days at a time.

As we headed back up the mountain toward home, the breeze turned into a stiff wind. Still, I hauled hay in wind before without losing any bales, so I didn't give it much thought. Then, about halfway home, traveling at forty-five miles per hour, we began to round a long sloping turn. Out of nowhere we were hit with one of those sixty-mile-per-hour gusts coming off the Divide and rushing down through the canyon we were in.

We were slightly broadside to the gust, and the combined speed of the truck and wind gust easily reached over a hundred miles per hour. Apparently, we must have been at just the right angle to the gust when it hit because the wind somehow got under the middle row of hay, lifted it out of the bed and dumped it and the top row of bales right in the middle of the road.

I didn't even have to look to see that we lost the load. The lurch of the truck when the bales fell off was so close to the feel of the lurch of Walter's truck when he lost his loads, that I immediately knew what happened.

As quick as I could I pulled onto the shoulder and backed up to where the bales lay in a pathetic heap. Some were still in the road, some were on the shoulder, some were in the ditch.

Tim, stifling a laugh as we pulled to a stop, looked over at me. "That apple didn't fall far from the tree."

He'd apparently read the book.

———

As I mentioned earlier, Walter wasn't a particularly chatty person. As a result, much of what I gleaned from him about horses during our time together came through watching how he did things. I also learned a lot from making and then correcting my own mistakes, (sometimes with his guidance, sometimes without) as well as through specific questions I might ask of him. Even when I did ask questions, however, most of his answers would be concise and usually without a whole lot of elaboration.

I hope folks don't misunderstand me here. I never got the feeling Walter was averse to answering my questions, and he certainly wasn't opposed to helping me when

I needed it. Rather, he was just a quiet guy. He was quiet with horses, he was quiet with people, he was quiet with dogs, cats, chickens, you name it. In fact, the loudest thing about him was his old pickup truck, a contraption that you'd always hear long before you'd see it.

Not only that, but as time has passed, I've come to appreciate the fact that with a lifetime of hard-scrabble ranching behind him, he probably saw our situation as more of a boss/employee type of deal rather than a teacher/student relationship. I was expected to know how to do the job he "hired" me for, and if there was something I didn't know (which was almost everything in the beginning) I was expected to figure it out. Figuring it out usually meant watching him do it, then copying what he did until I became proficient. If I couldn't figure something out, then he'd step in and help. Even then, it was usually just enough help to get me headed in the right direction before leaving me to it.

By learning in this way, I went from barely knowing which end of the horse to clean up after, to figuring out how to feed, water, groom, saddle, bridle, and ride in a little over a year. A year after that I picked up enough skill to start a young horse under saddle by myself. Mind you, I'm not saying it was the best starting job you ever saw, because I absolutely left plenty of holes that needed to be filled. But it doesn't take away from the fact that Walter had enough trust in me and my fledgling skills to at least let me try.

I've come to understand being a student of and through observation is just one more of those things I picked up from Walter that lives mostly in my subconscious. More times than not, especially in an organized learning situation such as my martial arts training or sitting in our friend Dr. Steve Peter's class on equine brain science, I will find myself sitting quietly, taking everything in that is being presented, often going through an entire class or series of organized classes before realizing I never once asked a question.

This type of observational learning often bleeds over into my own teaching, sometimes to the consternation of my students.

A few years ago, my wife Crissi and I, along with a couple of our student instructors, were teaching one of our ten-day intensive clinics. The way things are set up at the ranch where the clinics are held is a round pen is attached to one end of the large arena via a main gate; at the other end of the arena is the pen where we keep our cattle. For the most part, especially during the first few days of the clinic, most of the riders will work in or near the big arena. This day was no exception.

The one person not in the arena was Samantha, who was in the round pen with a young mare on which she only had a couple rides. From where I was in the middle of the arena, I watched as Samantha worked with the mare, getting her used to the idea of standing quietly next to a mounting block so a rider could mount.

There are several ways to teach a horse this skill, with some being more effective than others. Samantha was using a variation of a method that usually fits into the less effective category. I say this because what she was doing usually causes some confusion for the horse, which results in the horse trying almost everything *except* standing next to the mounting block. However, as I watched Samantha and her horse, it seemed clear that the little mare was actually picking up on what Samantha was asking.

Sitting on my horse, I watched the pair for several minutes before riding over so I could get a closer look. I sat several feet from the round pen and quietly watched as Samantha went about her business. From time to time, she glanced over her shoulder at me, usually with a sort of forced smile, but for the most part she just continued with what she was doing.

When I was watching from a distance, I noticed her movements and the direction she was giving her horse were smooth and flowing and her timing impeccable. But now her movements seemed a little abrupt, which was throwing her timing off and because of that her horse was starting to struggle with things that just a couple minutes ago seemed easy.

Samantha stopped everything she was doing and turned to me.

"You probably came over to tell me I'm doing everything wrong," she said, a hint of defeat in her voice.

The statement took me by surprise as nothing could have been further from the truth. In that moment I was learning, not teaching. I'd become so absorbed in what she was doing and how she was doing it that it didn't even dawn on me that my presence may have been interpreted as anything else.

"Not at all," I told her. "I was just interested in what you were doing and thought I could learn something."

"Really?"

As it turns out, with observational learning, every situation is a learning opportunity, and everything and everybody is both teacher and student.

Back in the summer of 2009, I took Crissi to where Walter's little horse ranch used to be. When I was a kid, it was in the middle of nowhere, a mile or so bike ride down a dirt road from my house at the edge of town. But in 2009, the entire area was in the middle of suburbia.

"The driveway to the ranch was right in here somewhere," I said as we drove down the smoothly paved road, past rows of identical houses and toward where the ranch once stood. I'd estimated the distance from the intersection we just drove past to where the driveway used to be based solely on the number of times I'd traveled it back in the day.

As we neared the location where I thought the driveway had been, we came upon a very nicely kept one-story retirement home tucked in amongst all the houses. It's half-circle driveway seemed to be in almost the exact spot where the ranch driveway was. I slowed the truck as we passed, pointing out to Crissi where Walter's driveway had been.

As we drove by, both of us looking at the retirement home driveway, we saw that it curved to the south, toward the front of the building. This curve in the driveway allowed for about a forty-foot-wide opening between the retirement home to the south and to where the rows of houses began again to the north.

Looking through this opening we could see the only area in the entire neighborhood that hadn't been developed. This opening, a field filled with wildflowers, reached all the way to where the east boundary of Walter's property used to be. This would have been the very back of his property when I was little and was distinguished by a narrow row of trees and bushes and a fence that I built one summer. The fence was gone, but the row of trees was still there. All the old ranch buildings were gone as well.

Wanting to get a closer look at the piece of ground Crissi had heard so much about, we drove a little farther and found another street that turned to the right. The street was a cul-de-sac with its south edge butting up against what would have been Walter's north fence line. We parked right near where the fence line would have been. There weren't any "No Trespassing" signs, so we walked onto what was once Walter's little horse ranch. I hadn't set foot on that ground for over forty years.

Of course, the property had been completely cleared decades before and there was no sign whatsoever that anything or anybody was ever there. Still, as we walked around, I pointed out to Crissi approximately where the barn, tack room, hay barn, and round pen used to be. I pointed out where the stalls and corrals once stood, and then we walked a little farther to the south, almost directly behind and about fifty yards away from the back of the retirement home we'd noticed on our way in.

I looked west, toward the building, then east, toward the row of trees that once made up the back boundary of Walter's property.

"There used to be a fence line right in here somewhere," I told Crissi. "It went from the road all the way back to that row of trees." I pointed toward the trees. "There was a pasture on the other side and gate back there somewhere." I pointed to my right.

"Are you sure it was *right* here?" she asked.

"Pretty sure. I built it," I said. "This fence line and the back fence. Walter had me replace them when they started falling down. I put the corner post in right up against the tree line. Needed to cut through a bunch of roots to get it deep enough."

She turned toward the trees and walked directly toward them, right along the line where I estimated the fence was.

"Where are you going?"

"There's got to be something left from back then," she said, determination in her voice. "It can't all be gone. Maybe there's a small piece of wire from the fence or something."

"It was a long time ago," I said, not wanting her to get her hopes too high.

Undeterred, she walked into the tree line, pushing undergrowth aside with her foot as she went. I followed behind.

"Where did you say this back fence was?"

"Right in here somewhere," I traced a line in the air with my hand indicating approximately where the fence stood. "The south fence would have been there." I traced another line in the air.

She walked past me to where she figured the two fence lines intersected and pushed more undergrowth aside with her foot. Within seconds, her foot bumped up against something solid. She reached down, moving the undergrowth aside before stopping. She stood up; a smile crossed her face.

"I found it!"

"What?"

"Your corner post!"

"What?"

"It's right here!"

Sure enough, against all odds, she'd found the corner post I'd planted all those years before. Time and the elements had taken their toll, and there wasn't much left of it. But there it was.

Crissi found the relic she'd been looking for. She took a picture of me standing with the post, and then we put it back where we found it. We covered it with undergrowth, took one last long look around, and went along our way.

Walter was a smoker. I'm not sure if he was a chain smoker, but he most certainly did his part to keep the tobacco industry in business. It was one of the things I remember most about him. One of the reasons it made such an impression was because he seemed to use lighting up as a way to create a brief pause in whatever was going on, or to form his thoughts before talking, or perhaps even process something he was observing.

If I'd ask him a question, and he didn't already have a cigarette lit, he would almost always light one before answering. If he was watching me work with a horse and want-ed to interject something, he'd light up before doing so. If he was sizing up a new or troubled horse, he'd light a cigarette. And I would be hard pressed to count how many times I saw him standing at that fence, the corner post of which Crissi found buried in the weeds, smoking a cigarette, watching the horses in the pasture on the other side.

In fact, one of the first things he did the first time we met (after he caught me sneak-ing into that south pasture so I could pet his horses) was light a cigarette.

Of course, I'll never really know if he used lighting a cigarette as an intentional pause or if it was simply a coincidence. What I do know is the connection of him pausing be-fore answering questions is something that rubbed off on me. Not to the point of me lighting up, seeing as how I never smoked. But the actual pause to gather thoughts before answering a question or before speaking or while observing something.

Every time he paused, I had to pause, which forced my preteen brain to slow down a bit. As time went on and I started getting used to his pauses, it also gave me a few extra seconds to mull the situation over as well. This not only helped me develop some semblance of patience, but more importantly, it offered me an introduction to the skills I would need to solve problems on my own. Sometimes all we need in order to come to a workable solution is just a few seconds of relief from thinking about it.

Back when it was just me working with horses on some ranch somewhere, it never really mattered how long it took me to ponder this situation or that. But once I began working with the public, whether for private individuals or during clinics, I started to become aware of how much time I would sometimes take to observe a horse-and-rider situation or answer a question. I say this mostly because some folks just couldn't help themselves from filling the dead air my momentary silence would create.

Many is the time during a clinic when someone, usually auditors, will ask a question about something they saw or something I'd said. In the couple quiet moments I use to help myself form a coherent answer, someone in the audience will often jump in and answer the question for me. In most cases, this input isn't anywhere near what my answer would have been, but before I can say anything about it, someone else will have added two cents, and then someone else will add two cents, and someone else will add another two cents. After several minutes of this I usually just go back to what I was doing before the question was asked without ever having gotten an opportunity to address the question at all.

The more we learn about science-based brain function in both horses and humans (something we will discuss in a little more detail later) the more we begin to see just how necessary those pauses can be to learning.

My guess is Walter gave very little, if any, thought to *how* a horse or person learned. Only that they did. And in a life based on decades of observation and trial and error, he more than likely found some things he did with horses worked better than others. I expect he realized at some point that allowing what we might now call "soak time" for both him and his horses, learning came easier and became more thorough. Over time, I believe, a slower, more thoughtful way of going with horses became a way of life for him, which he ultimately passed along to me, and which I now find myself offering to others.

The older I get, the more I can appreciate all those hours he spent standing next to that now long-gone south fence line, smoking cigarettes, and watching horses.

Harmony is a word that gets tossed around a lot in the horse world these days. For many, the word conjures up the idea of perpetual joy, happiness, and understanding in all our interactions with horses. It can also create a bit of angst during those inevitable times when joy, happiness, and understanding just aren't there.

When it comes to horses, harmony isn't about perpetual anything. It's about balance. Horses that understand how to do the things being asked of them or who aren't dealing with physical issues or unfortunate handling on a regular basis will usually develop a feeling of safety, which in turns allows them to achieve some semblance of emotional balance.

On the other hand, the more confused horses are due to pain, lack of consistency by their owners, lack of understanding on how to do their jobs and being forced to do them anyway, or perhaps because of an overabundance of unfortunate handling by the people they've been in contact with, the more out-of-emotional-balance horses may get.

Emotional imbalance usually causes fear in horses, which can turn into unwanted behavior brought on by horses feeling they must defend themselves. This emotional imbalance in the horse can, and often is, made worse by how the imbalanced horse's behavior is treated by a handler.

Defensive behavior in horses is often looked upon as aggressive behavior by a lot of horse folks. When handlers assume the horse is being aggressive, they will also assume the situation is adversarial. People not well versed in handling adversarial situations will usually flip into their sympathetic—fight, flight, or freeze—nervous system, the same place the horse has already gone.

Handlers in that frame of mind can't reason their way out of the situation very well. Instead, they will only be able to react to what is going on, usually after the horse's behavior has already occurred. Because of that, handlers are always behind in their responses to what the horse is doing, which only adds to the confusion that causes an escalation in the horse's behavior.

Please don't get me wrong here. I am not saying any of this as a judgment about people who have found themselves in this kind of situation. The truth is, everybody who has been around horses for any amount of time, myself included, has undoubtedly found themselves in the same, or similar situation as the one I just described. We should try to remember we're all doing the best we can at any given time and, hopefully, even those times when we get in over our heads can become learning opportunities that we can figure out how to avoid in the future.

Still, one thing that can make situations like I described even worse is the misguided idea prevalent in the horse world that horses are capable of respect or disrespect. They aren't.

Several years ago, while doing some research on equine brain science, I learned horses don't possess the part of the brain that allows for (among other things) understanding abstract concepts. These concepts would include good and bad, right and wrong, respect and disrespect, the ability to plan ahead, and so on. In other words, horse behavior has no value whatsoever to the horse. The only reason a behavior has value is because we put a value on it, not because the horse sees a value in it.

The only way horses will ultimately see value in a behavior is if they benefit from the behavior in some way. One of the ways they benefit is if they get a release for having done it. For example, a handler who moves out of the way (release) every time the horse steps into the handler's space can very easily and very quickly teach the horse to become "pushy."

Becoming pushy was not the horse's idea nor intention when moving into the handler's space the first time. All the horse was doing was offering an innocuous behavior that yielded an inadvertent reward. But the result was the horse learning a behavior we don't want. And yet a great number of horses that have been taught this behavior in exactly this way are deemed "disrespectful"—even though they are doing exactly what they have been taught!

Horse behavior is also directly attached to the way horses feel, and unlike humans, they can't distinguish between the way they feel and the way they act. A worried horse will act worried. A defensive horse will be defensive. A frightened horse will want to run, and if the horse can't run, the horse will fight. Understanding even this one basic function of a horse's brain can go a long way to helping us figure out why horses do the things they do, and how we can better learn to deal with them in a positive and productive way.

I bring all of this up because I think sometimes in our quest to have a harmonious relationship with our horses, we lose track of reality. And that reality is no matter how hard we try, or how much we wish it to be true, things just aren't always going to go the way we'd like. And it can happen to the best of us.

Walter made his living with horses. He did this mostly by buying, training, and then selling horses he would pick up at sales or that people didn't want anymore. Because he was buying mostly castaways and "killer" horses—ones bound for slaughter—many of these horses came with training issues, some of them substantial.

Back then, someone like Walter might have been referred to as a horse trader. Today he might be referred to as someone who rescues horses. I doubt he ever saw himself as either.

Most horse traders then and now buy horses with which they can turn a quick and easy profit. Some less-than-reputable ones use underhanded methods to get horses sold, such as drugging horses to temporarily change their temperament or hide a lameness. Walter didn't seem particularly interested in how fast he sold a horse, or if he made a profit on the sale, and I never saw him buy or sell horses that needed drugs to alter their temperament or hide physical issues.

Along those same lines, I'm not sure Walter saw what he did as rescuing horses, either. Many horse rescue organizations out there go out of their way to take in almost any horse regardless of training, soundness, temperament, or whatever. That is not a criticism, but rather just the way it is for a lot of rescues, and if they have the wherewithal to take care of all those horses properly, I'm all for it.

But that wasn't what Walter did. He looked for very specific internal qualities, if you will, in the horses he bought. Many was the time I saw him bypass horses that outwardly seemed to have everything going for them—pedigree, looks, size, training—for some undernourished-knock-kneed-pig-eyed-rafter-hipped-looking thing. Or he might buy the horses that were throwing themselves around inside their pens when Walter went to look at them, or the horses nobody could catch, or the ones standing with their heads in the corner of their stalls.

To this day I couldn't tell you what he saw in any of those horses, and he only offered an explanation a couple times, which I didn't really grasp anyway. What I do know is each one he picked out ended up being a willing horse most anybody could ride or work with.

After giving each of these horses time to settle in, usually anywhere from a few days to a few weeks or months, he would start working with them. Some settled right into his quiet and thoughtful way of working with them, with a good lot of those seemingly even drawn to what he had to offer.

But then there were a few others that, no matter how much decompression time he gave them or how quietly he offered information, just didn't seem to want to have anything to do with him or the situation. Some of these horses exhibited the types of defensive behavior I mentioned earlier that might be referred to as disrespectful by some folks.

These horses might charge if he went in the pen with them, some might swing their bodies into him if they were standing tied, some might kick in his direction as they ran past in a pen, some might offer to bite or rear. Still, Walter never used the word "disrespect" in relation to any of these behaviors. He did use a different word, though: "grouchy."

If a gelding was slinging his head and stomping his feet, Walter would say, "Looks like he's feeling a little grouchy today."

If a mare charged him, he'd quip, "Groucheeeee."

When a horse he was trying to catch would run from him he'd shrug and say, "He's just trying to get some of his grouch out."

If the behavior was big but nonthreatening, such as running mindless circles in a round pen, he might do something relatively minor to redirect what the horse was doing. This might mean stepping in front of the horse and slapping a lead rope on the ground, which would, in turn, get the horse to change directions, effectively getting the horse out of the mindless circling and helping the horse to mentally engage.

In other cases, when the horse's behavior was bigger and potentially much more dangerous, he would counter with something a little more firm and to the point.

I recall a gelding that'd been with us for a couple months called Cat, a name that matched his athleticism. The complaint Cat's previous owner had about him was he hated people. Seemingly true to form, the first time Walter went into the pen to work with him, Cat acted as if he was going to run away, only to wheel at the last second and charge.

"Now, now," I remember Walter saying in the tone of voice one might use to quiet a young child pitching a half-hearted fit.

Walter always carried a halter and rope in the crook of his arm whenever he worked with a horse, but especially when working with one he didn't know. This time was no exception. In the blink of an eye, he took the halter rope from the crook of his arm, flicked the end of it out toward Cat with the very end of it connecting with Cat's nose.

Cat slid to a stop just a few feet from Walter, who stepped slightly off to the side. Almost quicker than I could comprehend, Walter flicked the end of the rope just over, but not touching Cat's ears, brought it back, then flicked it again, tapping Cat on the shoulder with it. This caused Cat to wheel and gallop off in the other direction.

Cat reached the far corner of his pen in about seven strides, spun, and faced Walter. He threw his head in the air, eyes wide, and snorted.

"Okay," I heard Walter quietly say as he lit a cigarette. "That'll be enough of that."

The rest of that session, which to my recollection didn't last more than about a half-hour, started off with Cat being quite worried and cautious, but ended with him quietly approaching Walter and even reaching out and touching him with his nose.

It has taken me years to understand that what Walter had in his work with horses was *balance*. He was able to meet the horse wherever the horse was emotionally, then work outward from there. He also possessed an uncanny ability to keep the same level of calm regardless of the situation. It didn't matter if he was riding one of his long-time, well-trained saddle horses, or redirecting a struggling new horse like Cat, it all looked equally effortless for him. Walter always looked, sounded, and acted the same, and because of that was able to achieve amazing results with the horses in his care.

Having seen the way horses responded to him and his way of going, I knew if I was ever going to work with horses on my own, I would want to do the work the same way he did. A noble endeavor for sure.

What I slowly realized once I was on my own, however, was the universal truth that an effortlessness of skill is seldom easily achieved.

CHAPTER 3

A Blurry Path

"I'm always doing that which I cannot do,
in order that I may learn how to do it."

PABLO PICASSO

My grandmother's house was built in the late 1800s by her grandfather. It was a white, two-story Victorian on the banks of a large river and was surrounded by plum, peach, cherry, and apple trees.

It had three bedrooms upstairs that could be reached by climbing a narrow, slightly curved and creaking staircase that us kids were never allowed to use because it was too dangerous, although apparently not too dangerous for grownups, who used it all the time.

On the main floor was a large dining room, a smaller front room, in which there was an upright piano my aunt would play from time to time and where my grandmother would sit in the evening and watch Lawrence Welk. There was also a small sitting room, a fairly large kitchen with a walk-in pantry, and then all the way at the back of the house, a bathroom that was added on in the early 1900s.

It seemed like a castle to me at the time with its high ceilings, big windows, and stained hardwood floors and trim. In fact, the place was spacious enough to get up quite a little speed if you wanted to run "full blast" from the front room, through the dining room, through the kitchen and into the bathroom, all of which was a straight shot. This was a feat I only achieved once before being told in no uncertain terms by my grandmother that we didn't do that sort of thing in the house.

Our house was considerably less grandiose in contrast. Our family lived in about a nine-hundred-square-foot, one-story house with two small bedrooms, a tiny bathroom, small living room, and an equally small kitchen. Mom and dad were in one bedroom, my three brothers and I had the other bedroom, and my sisters slept on a foldout couch in the living room with their clothes in boxes on the floor of a tiny closet just outside the bathroom.

There were a lot of kids in our neighborhood, but there seemed to be an unwritten rule amongst the parents that no kids other than their own should ever be allowed in anybody else's house. As a result, not only did we all spend pretty much all our time playing outside, but it caused me to have an extremely narrow perspective of how big the inside of houses were, or could be.

To help solidify this perspective was the fact that all the houses in our neighborhood looked pretty much the same from the outside. Most were even painted the same colors, either a dirty off white or a sort of pale green. Ours was the latter.

Because of all this, my understanding from the time I was old enough to think until I was about twelve years old was that grandmothers' houses looked a certain way inside and out, and everybody else's houses looked another way. In other words, grandmothers lived in castles, families lived in hovels.

This all changed when I was thirteen years old. That was the year my parents decided the house I grew up in, the one that was only a short bike ride from Walter's little horse ranch, had become too small for us. And they weren't wrong. Us kids were all getting bigger, but the house wasn't.

So that year, like the Clampetts from the old Beverly Hillbillies TV show, we packed up our meager belongings and moved to a newly built and much bigger house in a completely different town some ten miles away.

The major upside of the move was the new house was three times as big as our previous home. It had double the number of bedrooms and bathrooms along with a much bigger kitchen and living room. There was also a two-car garage, which seemed like a bit of a waste, seeing as how our secondhand 1959 Buick Le Sabre hadn't ever been under any kind of covering, much less having the comfort of an entire building all to itself.

The downside to the move, at least for me, was it was now nearly impossible to get to Walter's place. Not only were we ten miles away, but there were only two roads that led out of the new town and in his direction. Both were busy highways with narrow shoulders, and neither were conducive to a safe bike ride.

As a result, my time with Walter effectively came to an end. I did make the effort to go see him a time or two that summer, but the twenty-mile round trip on a single-geared bicycle while cars and trucks whizzed dangerously close, honking horns as they passed, was a little more than even my perceived thirteen-year-old invincibility armor could withstand.

Along with the new neighborhood came new and additional interests. It was my eighth-grade year in school, and I met new friends, delved heavily into sports and schoolwork, and after seeing black-and-white concert footage of Creedence Clearwater Revival on TV, decided I wanted to be a drummer.

A friend from our football team owned a drum set he was selling for fifty dollars, so I got a weekend job bussing tables at a little diner where my older sister waitressed. I made enough money to buy the drums, taught myself how to play, and a few months later picked up a professional gig with a band called Jerry and the Jesters. The band consisted of Jerry (who was twenty-eight years old with six kids) and the Jesters. The Jesters were me and a friend named Gary who lived just down the street and kind of played bass. Gary (who was also self-taught) and I'd been getting together a couple times a week in my basement to play along with records. After a while we fancied ourselves pretty darn good musicians, which is why we felt confident enough to answer an ad Jerry posted on a music store message board.

It turned out Jerry fired the previous Jesters just a few days before, and because I could more or less keep a steady beat and Gary could more or less play in the proper key, along with the fact that Jerry had a long list of gigs starting as soon as that upcoming weekend, he hired us on the spot. Gary and I were both big for our ages, and so were able to get away with playing all the weddings and most of the bars Jerry booked.

During this time, it seemed like just about everything and everybody in my life was trying to lure me away from horses, and almost did until I turned sixteen and got my driver's license. It was then, while driving around in the car my parents upgraded to, a 1964 Oldsmobile, that I stopped into a fast-food joint and ran into a girl I went to grade school with named Jean. Jean and I had been classmates from the time we were in first grade until the time I moved away.

I'd always liked Jean. She was funny, smart, thoughtful, and tough when she needed to be. She had a wide variety of interests, but sports and animals seemed to be at the top of the list. Jean was even friends with a male wood duck that lived in the woods near her house. She could imitate the duck's whistle, and whenever she did, he would show up and follow her around, sometimes for just a few minutes, other times for most of the day.

Over time, and after months of us getting reacquainted through my many stops at the fast-food place, we started dating.

Jean owned a little gray mare named Tippy she trained herself and with which we always spent time whenever I was at her house. Although Jean was more or less "self-taught" when it came to horses, her way with Tippy was quite similar to the way Walter was with his horses. She didn't do things exactly like Walter, but what she did do had a very similar feel. It was soft, thoughtful, and effective.

It wasn't long before I found myself joining her and Tippy for all kinds of activities including trail rides, horse shows, and even sleigh rides in the winter, all of which gave me the opportunity to pick up learning about horses where I left off with Walter.

Jean and I dated all through high school and for another year or two after that. We did eventually go our separate ways when she went off to college to study to become a vet, and I went out on the road with a band, but we have remained close friends to this day.

The reason I bring up Jean and Tippy is because my time with them not only helped me reconnect with horses when I was starting to drift away from them, but more importantly, it helped me reconnect to a certain way of being with horses.

⌣

Over the next several years I found sporadic work with horses intermingled with my work as a traveling musician. This lasted until I was in my early twenties, at which point I started feeling the need to get back to working with and learning more about horses on more of a full-time basis.

I quickly found that jobs involving horses, especially for someone with my relatively limited experience, were in short supply. But I eventually found a seasonal position as a wrangler at a big livery operation just outside Rocky Mountain National Park.

I was one of twelve wranglers hired for the summer season. The operation owned over a hundred horses, including draft horses and ponies, and we worked seven days a week, twelve to fourteen hours per day, from May till the end of September. For that we were paid two hundred dollars per month, plus room and board.

When I arrived in May, one of the first jobs I was given was to help bring the horses off the 2500-acre pasture where they spent the winter. The pasture was in the foothills, some thirty miles from the ranch, and included large open meadows connected by rocky game trails and lots of steep ground dotted by heavily wooded slopes.

The spring gather was broken into four separate gathers, one per week for a month. The way each one worked was the boss would take a motorized three-wheeler (the forerunner of the much less dangerous four-wheeler of today) up into the pasture. He would round up whatever horses he could find that were relatively close and bring them back to the catch pen where the rest of us waited. Once in the pen, we saddled up what he'd brought in and headed back out to the pasture to gather whatever else we could find.

The horses we rode were what is commonly referred to as "dude" horses. That is, horses that even the most inexperienced rider could get along with, and during the summer months, they'd be trusted to carry these inexperienced riders on leisurely trail rides through the mountains. But at this point in the season and having not seen a human in close to nine months, most had gone a bit feral. As a result, the first several minutes of the gather were usually pretty lively for both horses and riders.

I would later learn that the boss used these spring gathers as a way to suss out the newly hired wranglers. One way to know if he liked what he saw was if he picked you for subsequent gathers. If he did, it meant he was confident in your skills. If he didn't, it meant he found something lacking.

Another way to know what he thought of your abilities was by the horse or horses he assigned to you for the summer. If he put you on one of the dude horses, then he had some questions about your skills. Assigning you an actual "guide" horse meant he was a little more confident in what you could do.

On this particular operation, most of the guide horses were either new horses recently purchased and unproven or established horses in the herd that would traditionally start the season with a little more energy than the typical guest could handle. In either case, the goal throughout the season was for the wranglers to ride the guide horses until they were safe enough for guests, at which point the horse would go into the string and the wrangler would be assigned a new guide horse.

In amongst the guide horses were two that no matter how much they were ridden, were just never going to be a dude horse. One of these horses was a sixteen-hand chestnut gelding named Sam Hill. The other was a big, black leggy Quarter Horse gelding named Roulette.

Sam Hill was one of the group that the boss rounded up with the three-wheeler at the start of that first gather.

"Mark, you can ride that big chestnut," the boss said, climbing off the three-wheeler after I closed the gate behind him once the horses were in the pen.

It took me a little time to get Sam Hill caught as he appeared to be a little put out at the idea of going back to work after his long winter vacation. So, after numerous high-speed laps around the large, rocky, catch pen, he finally let me get up to him and get him haltered. By the time I caught, groomed him, and was ready to saddle, everybody else was already saddled up and ready to go.

Instead of using personal saddles the boss had us use ranch saddles randomly plucked from their racks in the tack room prior to leaving the home place. Because I was the last one to get my horse caught, resulting in me being the last one to groom and thus get a saddle, I ended up with the saddle nobody else wanted—a seventy-five-year-old A-fork with a four-inch cantle and a fourteen-inch seat.

I generally ride in a fifteen-and-a-half-inch seat, fifteen-inch at a minimum, so to say the fourteen was a tight fit would be a bit of an understatement. Still, with it being the first time the boss would be getting a chance to see me ride, I didn't think mentioning it was the kind of first impression I wanted to present.

I lowered the stirrups before getting on and climbed aboard, but once on, found they were still too short. I was getting ready to climb down to lower them more when the boss called for me to stay mounted.

"We'll get 'em," he said, approaching with one of his former wranglers, a fellow named Smiley who'd come along to help out for the day.

I took both feet out of the stirrups as the boss adjusted my left stirrup and Smiley adjusted my right. Once he made his adjustment, the boss pulled down quick and hard on the stirrup to take the resulting slack from the adjustment out of the fender. This caused a loud popping sound as the fender leathers slapped together.

I think I mentioned that Sam Hill already seemed a bit agitated at the fact that we interrupted whatever plans he had for the day, and the slapping sound was the perfect catalyst for him to show us just how agitated he really was. The big gelding had a proper come apart as soon as he heard the noise, and the next thing I knew, Sam Hill and I were in the middle of a first-class bucking fit.

On the downside, the ground in the catch pen was littered with football sized rocks, and I was a long way from the ground on a tall horse made even taller with every jump he made. I was also without stirrups in a saddle much too small for me, which was admittedly a bit uncomfortable.

On the upside, I 'd gotten a good bit of practice riding bucking horses back when I worked with Walter. Most of these were horses we'd just gotten in and were supposed to be "quiet" and "broke to ride," and from the ground most certainly appeared to be that way. But once on their backs it was often another story.

I came off the first few of these horses back then and quickly learned to grab the saddle horn or whatever other leather I could get my hands on to help keep me on. I did have a little better luck after that—until Walter told me I was no longer allowed to grab leather. He said I was a good enough rider to stay with most of the horses he was putting me on, and if they bucked hard enough to get me off, then I deserved to be on the ground.

Over time I learned to find the "sweet spot" on horses that bucked—the place on their back that, almost no matter how hard they buck, doesn't really move very much. Once in that spot, and as long as the horse stays in a relatively straight line, the chances of staying on are pretty good.

With the football-sized rocks in the catch pen, the boss and everybody else watching, and being so far from the ground as motivation to stay aboard, I somehow found the sweet spot in that tiny saddle and without grabbing leather, was able to eventually ride Sam Hill all the way back down to a walk.

I rode Sam Hill for the entire gather that day. He was amazing. Absolutely no quit in him, went anywhere I pointed him, and no horse out there was able to outrun him. I rode him for the next week's gather, and for the two after that.

When it came time for the boss to assign horses for the summer, I just assumed I would be getting Sam Hill, but was surprised to find he gave Sam to another wrangler named Rob. Rob was the most inexperienced of all of us but extremely personable, fun to be around, great with the guests, and fearless on a horse—admittedly because he didn't know to be any different. Rob and Sam Hill got along great all summer long.

To my further surprise, the boss assigned me the big, leggy, black horse that was one of the last to come in on the final day of the gathers.

We all stood around in a semi-circle near the boss the day he assigned horses. He stood looking down at a clipboard, writing down horses' names next to wranglers' names as he made the assignments. One by one, everybody got their horses.

"Stephanie, you get Buttercup...Jeff, you get Lace...Justin, Kit...."

And so it went until everyone on the crew except me had an assigned horse. Then...

"Mark," just the hint of a grin escaped from under the brim of the boss's dirty straw hat. "I'm gonna give you Roulette."

As I understood it, Roulette was an Appendix Quarter Horse the boss picked up at a sale a couple years earlier. He'd been ridden through the sale ring by a cowboy, and from what I could gather, things didn't go well. Apparently, the bidding didn't go very high as a result, which is why the boss bought him. Back then, and probably still today, most dude operations tried to buy good horses cheap that with little or no work could just plug right into the dude string. Roulette wasn't one of those.

"He'll make a good horse for you if can figure out a way to get along with him," was the only other information or instruction I received.

Unlike Walter's little horse ranch where everything happened in a slow, methodical, and often somewhat meandering pace, this was a large, fast-moving operation, especially in the morning. It seemed everything about it was set up for speed and efficiency.

On this place there was one large barn that housed three separate "barns," all with tie stalls. There was what was referred to as the "main barn," which consisted of a large wood floor aisle with twelve tie stalls on either side of the aisle. There was also what we called the "back barn," which was under the same roof but separated from the main barn by an open wall and another walkway. It had also twelve stalls. Then there was what was referred to as the "kiddie barn," which had been added on to the main barn but was separated from the main barn and the back barn by the large tack room in between. There were ten tie stalls in it.

The tack room held saddles and bridles for all hundred-plus horses. The saddles were neatly arranged in alphabetical order on rows of saddle racks stacked five high. The bridles were hung in alphabetical order on the walls. A large door opened to the main barn from the tack room on one side of the tack room, and another large door opened into the kiddie barn on the other side of the tack room. Another smaller door opened into an attached office. Everything inside and out of the barn was always clean and tidy.

Around half past five in the morning, the horses would start gathering near a large gate at the bottom of their pasture that opened into an alley and led to the back door of the main barn. Next to this gate was a large hay barn and on the other side of the hay barn was another smaller gate where horses also gathered. This gate opened to another alley that led to the back barn and kiddie barn.

All of us wranglers would come in a half-hour later and immediately go to the grain bin, fill three wheelbarrows full of grain, take them to the middle of the main barn, the back barn, and kiddie barn, and with each wrangler filling a scoop in each hand, run to each tie stall and dump the grain into the small wooden grain feeders in each stall. The process was repeated until all the stalls had grain.

As the empty wheelbarrow was hurried away, one wrangler would run to each of the gates, large and small, and let horses in, making sure to let in only the number of horses that each barn could hold, and no more. Once in the barn, the horses would find an open stall and just put themselves in it, then go to eating.

While the horses would eat, each wrangler would claim a small section of the barn, with each section usually holding a minimum of four horses but sometimes as many as six. The wranglers would then halter each horse in their section using halters already tied with short halter ropes into the stalls. As soon as that was done, wranglers brushed their horses as quickly as they could. When the brushing was finished, the wranglers ran to the tack room and retrieved bridles that corresponded with the horses in their section.

By this time, two wranglers, one of which was always me, would already be in the tack room. As the wranglers bridled their horses, they would back the horses out of the stalls, call out each horse's name and hurry to the tack room door, usually two wranglers with one horse each forming two rows as they reached the door. The other tack room wrangler and I would grab the corresponding horse's saddle in one hand and a pad in the other and hurry out to the waiting horse.

The pad would go on the horse's back followed immediately by the saddle. On the off side of the horse, the wrangler would drop the neatly hung cinch while the person throwing the saddle would pull the equally neatly hung latigo from the near side, reach down take hold of the cinch, drop the latigo in the cinch ring, take a couple quick but snug wraps, and send them out the door. We would repeat this process until the barn was empty, and then repeat it again and again until all the horses on the place were saddled. We could average about a hundred head, fed, groomed, bridled, saddled, and tied to hitchrails outside, and barns and tack room swept and cleaned in about forty-five minutes.

When it came time for the boss to assign horses to guests, the same type of speed was used by the wranglers to retrieve the guest's horse. As soon as the guest's horse was announced, a wrangler would run to get the horse, then jog back to the assignment area slowing only to get the guest, who they'd take at a walk into the mounting area to get mounted while giving instructions for the ride. Once finished, that wrangler ran back to the assignment area and repeated the process.

Wranglers were usually assigned to a specific ride prior to the guests arriving, so when the entire group of riders was almost mounted, the assigned wranglers would break off helping in the mounting process and run to get their guide horses, which would normally be tied in an area relatively close to the front of the mounting area. The wranglers would jump on their horses, hurry to the front of the ride, and if the timing went well in the mounting process, as soon as the wranglers got to the front of the line, they were immediately ready to take the ride out.

I quickly learned there were a few steps in this process with which Roulette wasn't completely on board. The first was that he would allow himself to be haltered when he came into the barn first thing in the morning, but if he knew the halter was tied in, he would immediately pull back hard enough so either the halter rope or the halter would break. He also wouldn't stand tied at the hitchrails outside.

To be fair, he wasn't the only horse on the place that couldn't be tied. There were a handful of others. Rather than trying to fix the tying issues with these horses, which would have been a time-consuming process on a place where time was at a premium, the solution was to build a row of individual "fly-back" pens for them. There were about ten of these eight-by-six-foot covered pens where horses that were averse to being tied were kept after they were saddled in the morning. Roulette was in one of them.

Roulette also wasn't too crazy about letting me get on him when it was my turn to guide or accompany a ride. After taking him out of his pen he would trot circles around me as I adjusted his saddle and cinched it up, then trot more circles as I tried to get my foot in the stirrup in an attempt to get on.

I was younger then and still with some semblance of athleticism, so more times than not, and to save time, I would let him keep circling while I grabbed the saddle horn with my right hand and then pulled, jumped, and swung myself up into the saddle all in one fell swoop. Once in the saddle and I straightened him out, Roulette would half jump, half canter up to the front of the line where I would circle him to some semblance of a stop until the ride was ready to go out.

Once out on the ride, Roulette seldom settled into a nice walk, but rather we would spend most of our time slipping between some hapless combination of side-pass, passage, piaffe, and pirouette. The guests usually thought this display was quite something, often commenting on how great it looked, sometimes even garnering me some extra tip money. But it never felt good to me, and I'm sure it never felt good to Roulette, either.

The whole thing with Roulette ate at me from the start, and the longer it went on, the worse I felt. During my time with Walter, the majority of what we did was work toward finding ways to help troubled horses feel better. Because of that, knowing Roulette was unhappy was one thing, but riding him day after day in that state of mind without ever trying to help him was another.

With the rigorous daily schedule, the boss wasn't too keen on anybody riding or working with any of the horses outside of work hours. For that reason, I asked if it would be okay if I spent a little extra time with Roulette during our lunch breaks, and he agreed.

Our lunch routine was run about the same as the morning routine. The stalls were grained and horses let into the barn in shifts until everybody was fed, watered, and back out on the hitch rails. The one exception was the horses in the fly-back pens, including Roulette. Those horses stayed in their pens at lunch time where grain was brought to them, and they always had a bucket of water available.

Once all the horses were tended to, the wranglers would then sit down for lunch. Lunch breaks lasted between one-and-a-half and two hours, depending on what kinds of rides were scheduled in the afternoon. This meant if I didn't waste any time getting my lunch down, I would have anywhere from forty-five minutes to an hour to spend with Roulette before guests started showing back up.

Having eaten, I made my way around the front of the barn, past the guest assignment area and around the corner, which opened up into a large open area next to where all the kids' horses were tied and beyond which were the fly-back pens. Along the way I thought back to my time with Walter. On several occasions, when he would very first begin to work with a troubled horse, I asked him the same question: "How do you know where to start?"

He always gave me some variation of basically the same answer: "The horse will let you know."

Admittedly, that answer never really made much sense to my twelve-year-old self, and as I made my way toward Roulette's pen, it didn't seem to be of much help, either. But then something interesting happened. As I turned the corner and headed across the open area toward the fly-back pens, I looked up at Roulette and saw he was standing quietly in his pen. It was the first time I could recall Roulette ever standing quietly in his pen, especially when I was approaching.

I stopped for a minute while I tried to figure out what the difference was. Of course, the obvious difference was there wasn't a ride going out so there was the absence of all that activity. But there seemed to be another, perhaps more subtle difference. I wasn't charging up to the pen in a hurry to get him out and get to work.

I started toward his pen again and, a bit to my surprise, he stayed quiet the whole time. I went in the pen, took his bridle from the saddle horn and put it on him. I then took him out of the pen and with him still standing quietly, I adjusted his saddle and tightened the cinch. It was here he began to get a little nervous, so I walked him around until he quieted again, loosened the cinch, took the bridle off, and put him back in his pen.

I stood there for several seconds not knowing quite what to think about what just happened. It was literally the quietest I'd ever seen him. That included how he acted when we brought him off winter pasture, how he was during the morning feeding and saddling routine, anytime I tried to get on or ride him, how he was on the trails, and even the unsaddling routine at the end of the day. While I stood there, he turned and took a long drink from his water bucket, lifting his head when he finished. He let some of the water fall from his mouth while swallowing the rest, then let out a quiet sigh and nonchalantly glanced over at me.

Not knowing quite what to do next, I simply walked away. I went back across the open area and past the kids' horses all tied to the hitch rail. I turned the corner around the front of the barn and past the guest assignment area to a bench on the porch in front of the barn and sat down.

"The horse will let you know," kept running through my mind. But it couldn't be that simple, could it? Was Roulette really trying to tell me something here?

I sat for what seemed like a long time, although I doubt it was more than five minutes before getting up and heading back to his pen. I watched him closely as I approached, trying to move at the same speed and intensity I used the previous time. Once again, Roulette stood quietly while watching me come up. I again went in the pen, put his bridle on him, took him out, adjusted his saddle and cinched him up.

This time he stood calmly so I walked him around a little, then stopped and tried to put my foot in the stirrup. That seemed to be a bridge too far for him and he started to worry—a lot. I walked him around until he was quiet, then stood next to him, thinking. Had Walter been there, he would have no doubt lit a cigarette, letting out a long exhale before saying or doing anything.

The rhythm and timing of that old familiar cigarette-lighting pause washed over me, and in that moment, I had a thought. Actually, it was more like a question: What part of me raising my leg did Roulette not like? I lifted my leg so quickly and he reacted so fast that I didn't have any idea what part of the process of me lifting my leg caused him the problem. Was it my foot getting close to the stirrup? Was it me bending my knee, was it my knee getting close to his side? I had no idea. But I wanted to find out. So, while standing next to him, I tried again, this time much, much slower.

After a several attempts and resets, and with Roulette's help, I was eventually able to figure out exactly where his worry was coming from. It wasn't bending my knee or getting my foot close to the stirrup or my knee close to his side. The issue was happening way before that. In fact, it was way, *way* before that. The thing that was triggering his worry was happening before I even thought about picking my foot up off the ground. To make matters worse, it was something I hadn't even realized I was doing.

After numerous attempts and slowing myself down more after each one, I finally came to the realization that every time I *thought* about lifting my leg, I first unconsciously pinched the outside seam of my jeans between my thumb and index finger, slightly lifting the denim off the outside of my leg.

That was the thing that started him worrying.

Over the next several minutes, and to make sure that was the problem, I made a variety of changes to my initial behavior, either eliminating the seam pinch, or adding it back in. Each time I eliminated it, he would let me lift my leg without much of a fuss, providing I did it slowly enough. Each time I pinched the seam, no matter how slowly or in what form I did the pinch, his worry immediately escalated.

Trial and error over the next several minutes made it clear that as long as I didn't do the pinch, we could make some headway. But if he even thought my hand was heading toward that seam, all bets were off.

By the time lunch was over, he let me get my foot in the stirrup and even get on without him feeling like he wanted to take off. It was the first time since I first started riding him that he actually seemed okay with me getting on his back.

Over the next several days and weeks, I made more adjustments in the way I handled Roulette, most of which just boiled down to slowing down in everything I did with him. This even bled over into the morning feeding and saddling routine, as well as the unsaddling routine. If Roulette came in in the morning and wasn't in my section, I would switch with the wrangler whose section he was in, taking a little extra time to groom and bridle him. When he came to the tack room door to be saddled, I went through the process with him with more care and deliberation.

Most importantly, when it came to getting him out when it was time for us to guide a ride, I would hurry going to get him as was expected of all the wranglers, but I'd always slow to a walk when I got to within about thirty-five feet of his pen. As long as I did that, then took my time bridling, adjusting his saddle and cinching him up, and, of course, never touching the seam of my jeans while slowly lifting my leg, he would stand quietly and let me get on. We could then meander our way to the front of the line instead of lurching and jumping all the way there, and once out on the trail, our behavior while guiding rides became considerably less ostentatious than it was previously.

Don't get me wrong, there were still plenty of things that we needed to spend time on before we were a solid team, but as the summer went on, and if I at least made the effort to try to listen to what Roulette had to say, our good days well outweighed our bad ones.

During my time with Walter, I always followed his lead on what it might take to help a troubled horse feel better, and during that time I basically just shadowed what he did without really understanding the overall impact it was making. Looking back, I know now that I never felt a personal, or internal connection to what I was doing or even what was being done. Working with Roulette was my very first *real* taste of what it meant to use what little skill I possessed to create a positive change in the way a horse felt…and doing it because it was what was best for the horse, not necessarily because it was the best thing for me, although that certainly became a side effect.

In short, that summer with Roulette was my first ever effort—both inside and out—where I finally took the time to truly consider the horse. And for that, I am forever grateful.

One last thing, for those interested in how Roulette got his name…

As the boss told it, a few months after he bought Roulette, he tried to use him on one of the spring gathers. He apparently ended up coming off him three out of the five times that Roulette went to bucking. He called him Roulette from that day on because he said getting on him could be like playing Russian Roulette as to whether he would break in half or not.

I always appreciated the fact Roulette seemed to have moved past that particular character trait by the time he and I worked together.

CHAPTER 4

The Clouds Part

*"You must understand that there is more
than one path to the top of the mountain."*

MIYAMOTO MUSHASHI

After my time at the dude operation was up, I found myself getting day work on a couple cattle ranches, working as a teamster on another place that still did all their ranch work with horses, doing some outside training and colt starting for folks, and eventually, I was hired on as livery manager at a guest ranch not far from town.

In the years prior to me getting the job, this particular operation had the dubious distinction of being the leading cause of summertime accidents, injuries, and hospitalizations in the entire area. At least once a week some guest would end their trail ride with a jaunt in an ambulance or helicopter.

During my interview for the job, the assistant general manager of the place, a guy named Jeff, told me they were looking for someone to "right the ship," as their membership in the prestigious Dude and Guest Ranch Association was in jeopardy, specifically due to their dismal horse operation. It was early April with the summer season right around the corner, and I got the distinct impression he was under some pressure to get someone hired and get the place up and running sooner rather than later.

Part of my interview included a tour of the entire ranch. The main building was a combination conference center, guest lodging, employee housing, housekeeping center, maintenance building, and office center for the managers who took care of the various departments on the ranch. It was a massive log building—at the time, the largest log structure in Colorado, although I believe it's now been dwarfed by much bigger and more opulent complexes.

One of the first places Jeff took me during the tour was out to the front portico, a peaked roof held up by six large log uprights big enough for at least four cars to get underneath at the same time. We walked over to one of the uprights, where he pointed to a large, jagged gash in the log.

"You know what this is?" he asked.

"Someone hit it with a car?"

"No," he replied. "Last summer the livery manager was taking guests on a hayride when the team ran off. They came barreling up the hill," he pointed to the long, upward sloping driveway leading into the parking lot we were in, "and at a dead run, one horse went on this side of this log, the other went on that side."

"Oooh…" I heard myself say.

He turned from the upright and motioned for me to follow. "It's just one of the many reasons why he isn't here anymore."

We made our way through the parking lot, around melting piles of dirty snow and past the afore-mentioned hay rack, also partially buried in snow. Jutting precariously from one of these dirty snowbanks was the long metal tongue that would have separated the horses pulling the wagon. It was bent upward at a sharp right angle and remnants of the broken wooden yoke were still attached to the heavy metal ring at the end of the tongue. The eveners the horses would have been attached to were hopelessly bent as well, as was the entire metal steering mechanism in the wagon's undercarriage.

We walked down a long snow-packed trail, past a small water treatment plant, and into an area of what might have been a decent horse facility at one time, although it seemed clear those days were long past. Most of the fences and hitchrails were down or completely missing. Small piles of manure left over from the previous summer dotted the ground where the snow melted. Two much larger piles, both about six feet tall and eight or nine feet in diameter were heaped up not far from the front of the run-down barn, the front door of which stood wide open.

Snowmobiles stranded in patches of dirt sat like beached whales in what was probably a large dry lot corral just uphill from where the barn sat, and it looked like there may have been some smaller pens on the other side of the barn, but it was hard to tell for sure.

"From the records we have," Jeff said as we walked through the big open door, "this building is over one hundred and twenty years old."

Just a few feet inside the door I came to a stop, mostly because it would have been impossible to go any farther. The floor was littered with truck parts, old saddles, and bridles, tires, rusted water tanks, rat-eaten saddle blankets and pads, and in a pile off to the side was the torn-up, draft-horse harness that no doubt was involved in the hayrack accident.

"This is the tack room," he said, jerking a dilapidated plywood door open. It was only partially hung, and the bottom of the door dragged in protest across the old wooden floor, finally stopping altogether and leaving no more than about a foot-and-a-half space for us to get through.

The tack room was only a room in the literal sense, in that it had four walls, a ceiling and a floor. There was the door we came through, and another plywood door that opened to the outside front of the barn, but other than that it didn't have much going for it. A few saddles, such as they were, hung on racks on the walls with bridles hung on some of the saddle horns. Some of the bridles had reins on them, some didn't. Another pile of battered and rodent-eaten saddle blankets and pads sat scattered on the floor nearby.

"Where are the horses?" I asked.

"Horses?" He seemed surprised by the question.

"Yeah. Any chance I can see them?"

"They're out on winter pasture, about ten miles away," he said. "You want to see them?"

"If that's all right."

"Yeah…I mean, sure." There seemed to be more than a little hesitancy in his voice. "Is it a problem?"

"Not at all," he said, leading me back through the plywood door we just came through. "It's just, we've had several applicants come in, but they all backed out after seeing this place." He waved his arm to encompass the inside of the barn. "Nobody's even asked about the horses."

The ranch owned thirty-seven head, most of which were spread out in a high mountain valley owned by a neighboring ranch. Because they were so spread out, I was only able to get a good look at about the ten or so that were hanging around the well-built corrals and a large water tank with ice chunks floating in it near the caretaker's house. None of them would let me get close.

Back at the ranch, Jeff and I finished up the interview, which ended with him making an offer, and which I accepted—under one condition. That I would have total control over the entire horse operation. That would include hiring employees, buying and selling of horses, rebuilding the horse facility, how the program would be structured, and how rides would be scheduled.

Excusing himself, he got up from behind his desk and left the room, returning about fifteen minutes later with the general manager, a slightly heavy-set, bespectacled and gregarious fellow by the name of Boyd, who was dressed in a denim shirt and jeans.

"So why do you want this job?" Boyd asked, getting right to the point following our introduction.

"I think there's a lot of potential here," was my answer.

"And you think you could bring out that potential?"

"I'd like to try."

The room fell silent for a few seconds.

Boyd and Jeff glanced at one another, then Boyd nodded.

"Nice to meet you," he said, shaking my hand before leaving the room and closing the door behind him.

Jeff sat down behind his desk and let out a sigh.

"How soon could you start?"

I was on the job the following week and quickly found that having potential is one thing but finding a way to achieve that potential is quite another. Getting the facility in order was pretty cut and dried and consisted mostly of cleaning up and some basic construction and fence building. I did have some help in the form of a wrangler from the previous year who stayed on through the winter as a housekeeper. Her name was Carol, and she was not only a good hand with horses but a hard worker as well.

As the two of us went about the business of getting the facility put back together and organized, Carol would regale me with harrowing stories from the previous season. As I listened, I couldn't help but wonder how things were allowed to get so far out of control.

To hear Carol tell it, a horse, wrangler, or guest would be involved in some sort of accident almost every day. Some of these were minor, while others were much more serious. Broken limbs, concussions, cuts, and abrasions were apparently a common occurrence, so much so that the first aid kits each wrangler carried in their saddle bags had been replaced three and four times by the end of the summer.

On one hand, I found the information quite disturbing. On the other hand, I figured the only place we could go from there was up.

After a few weeks of working twelve-hour days, the barn and area surrounding it were back in shape. We completely rebuilt the tack room, modeling it somewhat after the much larger and very efficient tack room from my previous dude-ranch job, including orderly, handmade wooden saddle racks and a wall full of hooks for bridles. There was also a separate spot near the door leading into the barn designated specifically for saddle blankets and pads.

I built and installed two Dutch doors to replace the flimsy plywood doors, one inside the barn from the tack room to the inside aisleway, the other for the outside front entrance into the tack room. I also built a small porch for the front door of the tack room. We then put a fresh coat of paint on the front of the barn, rebuilt or replaced all the corral fences and built designated mounting and hitchrail areas.

At the same time all of this was going on, I was given a folder containing information on the six people that'd been hired to work as wranglers for the upcoming summer. These were not people I hired, but rather were hired by Jeff prior to me becoming the manager. Of the six on the list only two had actual horse experience, Carol, and a college student from back east named Linda.

I went to Jeff and explained that if we were going to create a positive change in the horse program, at the very minimum we would need people who actually knew something about horses. To that end, I told him I voided the contracts of the inexperienced people he hired and contacted three very experienced people I wrangled with at my last job and hired them instead. I still needed one more wrangler but was able to fill that spot by going through some already submitted applications.

While basically firing nearly the entire wrangling crew just weeks before we were scheduled to open raised eyebrows with Jeff and Boyd, what I did next nearly lost me my job entirely.

Once the facility itself was put back together, it was time to bring the horses in and see what we had, and as it turned out, what we had was not good. Of the thirty-seven saddle horses the ranch owned, only four were suited for the job we needed them for. The rest were either too old, too crippled, completely untrained, or just outright broncs.

With only two weeks to go before the first guests were to show up for their trail rides and precious little time to do any real work with the horses we owned, I was forced to make a decision. Do we go into the season with these horses, which clearly had not worked in the past, or do we do something different?

Another time, under different conditions or in a better situation, I might have tried to give the horses more of a chance, see if we could come to some understanding with them, get them on board and maybe even help them relax into the job. But it wasn't another time or under different conditions. The bottom line was changes needed to be made, and they needed to be made right away.

I sold every horse on the place except for the four I felt were going to work out and a few of the older horses I thought might make good kids' horses for short trail rides. I then used the money from the sale of the horses to lease experienced dude horses from a big outfit that specialized in supplying horses to various dude ranches around Colorado. All the horses we leased came with shoes, saddle, bridle, and saddle pad and all were guaranteed to work in our program. If for some reason they didn't work out, they could be exchanged for another horse that would. It was a win-win as far as I was concerned, and one I'd hoped would be the positive turning point our situation needed.

However, between selling the horses and just before the leased horses were delivered, I literally got called on the carpet in Boyd's office. It was an attractive red-and-teal Southwest-looking throw rug sprawled out on the floor in front of the large oak desk he sat behind, but that didn't make it any more comfortable when I was standing on it.

"You sold the horses?" he exclaimed, even before I could close the door behind me.

"Not all of them."

"How many?"

"Twenty-eight."

"That's the whole herd!"

"We kept nine."

"We can't run a summer horse program with nine horses!"

This was the first chance I had to go over the situation with Boyd as he'd been out of the office for the past week. Once I explained the plan and the reasons behind it, and more importantly, that the leased horses were being paid for from the sale of the herd so there weren't going to be any out-of-pocket expenses, Boyd seemed to calm down a bit.

"Can you guarantee these horses are going to be better than the ones we had?"

"Not yet," I said. "But I can guarantee they won't be any worse."

The horses and most of the wranglers showed up the next day, with the horses being delivered in a tractor-trailer out on the shoulder of the highway in front of the ranch. After checking the horses over as they were unloaded and then gathering all the tack that came in the back of a pickup that accompanied the semi, we brought all the horses up to the barn and corrals.

Normally, I would have given both the horses and wranglers a day to rest and settle in, but we didn't have the time. By late morning, all five of us were mounted and with Carol being the only one who knew the trails, she took the lead.

The ranch was at an elevation of over 9500 feet and even though it was mid-May, the trails still had some snow on them, especially in the trees, most of which were lodgepole and ponderosa pine. The higher we went, the more snow we ran into. As a result, we were only able to get on four trails out of the seven or eight we would be using on a regular basis throughout the summer.

As soon as we returned from one ride, we'd saddle up another five horses and take them out, then another five after that, and so on. By the end of the day, we had ridden all but eight of the new horses and all were exactly as advertised. They were all good solid trail horses with a handful of them suitable for kids and even three or four suitable for guide horses.

The wranglers used our time on the trail to get to know one another, joke around a bit, and tell stories of their past horse experiences. They also used the time to give the horses they rode names, seeing as how none of the leased horses came with names so far as we knew.

The two wranglers from back east showed up for work the next day, and after going through what would be our new summer-long morning routine of feeding, grooming, bridling, and saddling, all the wranglers went back out to further familiarize themselves with the horses and trails.

Later that day I met with all the wranglers to lay out the philosophy of our program, which boiled down to one simple thing. Safety.

I stressed that our primary job was the well-being of our guests, our horses, and ourselves, with the guests being at the top of that list and the rest a very close second. We were professionals, and we needed to conduct ourselves as such. To that end, there would be specific guidelines to the way we conducted our rides.

For instance, two wranglers would be assigned to any ride in which there were more than four guests. The "drag" wrangler's job was to keep an eye on everything and everybody from the back of the line forward, the "lead" wrangler would keep an eye on everything and everybody from the front or the line back. This way, we could hopefully head off any potential accidents before they happened.

While keeping an eye on things would be important, an even bigger key to keeping things safe on the trail would be keeping the overall stress level of the horses to a manageable level. One way of doing that was us getting to know the horses themselves. We needed to figure out their strengths and weaknesses, then have them do what they were good at and avoid the things they weren't. We would learn which horses got along and which ones didn't, then make sure the ones that got along were always near each other on rides.

If horses started to show signs of fatigue, soreness, or pain of any kind, they were to be taken out of service and tended to either by us, a vet, chiropractor, or possibly just given a few days off to rest and recuperate.

And last but certainly not least, we would train and handle our horses as quietly and effectively as possible. We would then show the guests how to ride them in such a way as to maintain that consistency, which in turn would help to preserve our herd's overall emotional balance.

I hadn't really thought about it at the time, but what we were doing was an experiment based almost exclusively on a philosophy about working with horses that I'd gleaned from Walter and tried to replicate in my horsemanship ever since. That is, horses just seem to do better when we can help them understand what's going on—regardless of the situation we put them in.

The result of the experiment was not only that we took out a record number of riders during our inaugural four-month season, but we also ended up with the ranch's first ever no-accident season as well. We did well enough financially to expand the herd from thirty-seven horses our first year to fifty the next—all were horses we purchased, including two (and ultimately three) teams of draft horses we did hayrides with in the summer and sleigh rides in the winter. The third year we added to our herd yet again, increasing our numbers from fifty to seventy-five, and we expanded our program to include lessons, mini-clinics, and advanced trail rides in which we did some trotting and cantering.

I stayed at the ranch for a total of three years, all the while maintaining the original philosophy with our horses of building trust and understanding through quiet, effective handling. During that time, we ended up taking out over 17,500 riders while at the same time continuing to maintain our no-accident record.

A few years later while working at another place starting colts, I was contacted by the owner of the dude ranch next door to the one I'd left (the two ranches shared a common fence line.) It turned out he was starting to have some of the same issues with accidents that the other ranch had prior to me getting hired on. He offered me the position of ranch foreman to see if we could get his horse operation squared away.

We basically implemented the same philosophy and guidelines for his horse program that we had used at the neighboring ranch, and ended up with pretty much the same results. The only difference was in the five years that I was his ranch foreman, we did actually have one rider come off. Or to be more precise, one person tried to get on but never made it. Not because the horse did anything she wasn't supposed to, because she never moved. But rather because the guy was wearing jeans way too tight for the activity and was simply unable to swing his leg over the mare's back. When a wrangler went to help him get on, the man's right thigh hit the cantle of the saddle, his left foot slipped out of stirrup, and he fell unceremoniously onto his backside in the dirt, ripping his jeans and spraining his thumb in the process.

So ended our perfect safety record.

The thing I learned from my time as a wrangler on the big dude outfit was there are a *lot* of little variables and moving parts associated with a well-run horse operation. I also saw firsthand how quickly things can come off the rails when any one of those variables and moving parts doesn't work as it should. So, while managing dude strings of my own, I figured the best way to mitigate those kinds of unfortunate issues was to get everything and everybody heading in the same direction, as it were. This meant I needed to figure out what our objective for the program was going to be, then reverse engineer from there to develop all the pieces and parts we would need to achieve that objective.

For me, the focus was always the safety of everybody and everything we came in contact with—guests, horses, wranglers, and property, among other things. I just assumed that the best way to get things moving on that path was when, first and foremost, our horses felt safe. I just couldn't help but feel if our horses felt good about their lives in general that it would take a tremendous amount of pressure off us to get those other little variables and moving parts just right all the time. It was for that reason we implemented all the handling and training procedures for both horses and wranglers, and to some extent, even the guests.

Along with that, however, I believe a lot of our success was also due to the way we chose both our horses and our wranglers in the first place. We spent a great deal of time making sure the wranglers we hired and horses we brought into the program had (at the very least) not only the basic skills they would need to do the job, but also the temperament it would take for them to be successful in that job. Having done everything we could to set ourselves up for success, including the long hours and hard work that come along with the running of that kind of operation, it was then quite rewarding when we not only achieved the desired outcome, but kept it going over an extended period of time.

Looking back, I can see just how much of what I did during those years began with the example Walter set on how to develop and maintain a healthy atmosphere with horses. He always focused on the horse's emotional and physical well-being, and that certainly played a huge part in the way I approached what I did back then, and as it continues to do in what I do today.

My time working on the dude ranches taught me it didn't really matter if we're working with one horse in our backyard or a hundred horses on some big operation somewhere. More times than not, by simply putting our primary focus on helping horses understand and feel good about what is being asked of them, everything else has a much better chance of just falling into place.

CHAPTER 5

The Art in the Art

*"It takes great courage to pick up a sword, it
takes even greater courage not to use it."*

AUTHOR UNKNOWN

Years ago, I bought a seventeen-year-old ranch horse by the name of Mouse.
Mouse had endured many years of unfortunate handling that caused him to
be pretty troubled around humans in general and strangers in particular. He was
worried about being caught, he didn't like to be saddled or tied or groomed or ridden. He didn't like people touching him or approaching him or moving around him
in almost any way.

In fact, the list of things he didn't like was much longer than the list of things he
did. Even so, and to his credit, he would always try to do what was asked even though
it would trouble him, most likely because he learned over the years that those things
were just part of his job. He just didn't like any of it much.

I got him from a friend who bought him a year or so before as a horse to practice his
roping with. My friend, by his own admission, didn't try to do much to help him
with any of his troubles. By the same token, he hadn't made any of them worse, either.

I saw him ride Mouse on several occasions and watched firsthand the kind of worry the gelding packed around. But still, there was just something about him that resonated with me, and when my friend decided to move on to a little more refined roping horse, I bought Mouse from him.

Having just retired my good saddle horse Buck from traveling, Mouse hit the road as my primary clinic horse. I realized almost from the start that the last thing Mouse needed was more training. You know, the kind of training some folks feel the need to use to help a troubled horse feel better. Mouse had plenty of training and more than enough handling in his life. What he hadn't been given much of was time to learn how to be okay when he was around people, and particularly when someone was on his back. Luckily for me, time was something I had plenty of.

Don't get me wrong here. I am in no way suggesting working with horses to help them feel better when they're worried or troubled is a bad thing. When done properly, as I mentioned in regard to work in the dude strings, it can be an extremely effective way of getting horses to understand and ultimately be okay with the tasks they'll need to know to perform their jobs. But as I said, in Mouse's case, more training didn't really seem like the best course of action.

Instead, I made the decision early on that I would simply work with and ride him the way I wanted him to go. What that meant for the two of us was I wouldn't necessarily ignore the things that bothered him or behavior he offered up that I wasn't looking for, but by the same token, I wouldn't really put much energy into those things either. In other words, I didn't make a big deal out of anything he offered that I didn't want. Instead, I mostly just redirected the things I didn't want as a way to turn them into the things I did. This took on a variety of different looks depending on the situation and the behavior he exhibited, but ultimately, the end goal was always the same. I wanted him to see I could be depended upon to help and guide him when he was troubled, instead of putting more pressure on him by trying to *train* the trouble out of him.

This wasn't really a new concept to me. To be honest, it was an idea I literally grew up with. As I've mentioned, when Walter purchased "throwaway" horses at various auctions, he would work with them, getting what he would call "the bugs" out, then ultimately resell them. Again, today he would possibly be considered a horse rescuer, but I don't believe he ever looked at it that way. For him, it was simply a way for him to make a living (meager as it may have been) with horses.

While I do remember him using specific training techniques with some horses from time to time, most of what he did was just work with what the horse present-ed and try not to make too big a deal out of anything. I look back on how and what he did back then, and the positive results he was able to get from horses that, quite frankly, were sometimes a little scary, and even today I marvel at the effectiveness of his simplicity.

I realize now what he was actually doing was developing trust between him and his horses, the kind of trust that can really only be achieved by taking the time it takes to build a relationship based in understanding—not the kind of manufactured and often tenuous trust that sometimes occurs through sheer repetition of technique. First and foremost, however, I believe it was his way of getting to know his horses (and them, him). And when I say he got to know them, I mean he *really* got to know them—from the inside out. He understood what made each individual horse tick, what the horse liked and didn't like, the horse's idiosyncrasies and mannerisms and most of all, the specific things each horse did to try to communicate with a handler or rider. By tru-ly getting to know his horses in this way, Walter was then able to get to the heart of what was *really* bothering them, then work with them at that level. After that, getting horses to *want* to work with him was easy. Spending time with his horses like this eliminated the need for him to assume or guess or speculate what was going on with them. He *knew* what was going on with them.

When I first bought Mouse, I didn't actually plan on working with him in this way. In fact, I really didn't have any plans at all on how I would work with him. But within a very short period, this direction not only seemed the best option, but really the only one.

Oddly enough, however, making the decision to work with him in this way was one I *felt* rather than *thought*, or, perhaps, maybe a better way to describe it would be that it was an *instinctual* decision. It just seemed like the best way to go. Either way, for Mouse, it ultimately turned out to be the right decision. Not only did Mouse's troubles drop away one by one over time, but he also became an extremely responsive and willing partner, whether we were working cattle, riding through the mountains, roping, or coaching riders during a clinic.

Still, one of the many things that Mouse struggled with, at least initially, was knowing where to be in relationship to the people around him. Even when leading him, if he became worried, he would either try to run away from people or he'd run them over, and there didn't seem to be much middle ground about which option he would choose or when.

Early on in our relationship, I showed him what his boundaries should be when he was around people. Again, we accomplished this mostly by directing what we didn't want and turning it into what we did. Anytime he would get worried when I was leading him and shy into or toward people, I would guide him into a position in line and at least an arm's length behind me. If he would get worried and offer to come over me, I would again redirect him into a position in line and at least an arm's length behind me. Within just about an hour's time spread out over a couple days, he figured out his boundaries and in doing so, became much more relaxed whenever he was led.

At one point just a couple months after I'd gotten him, I was leading him and another horse through a six- or seven-foot-wide alley between a horse trailer and a white plastic fence. Behind us and slightly off to one side was my assistant, also leading two horses. As we neared the end of the alley that then turned into a large open driveway, a rabbit jumped out of the tall grass growing under the fence. Surprised, Mouse jumped forward, toward me, but stopped short of the boundary we'd worked on. In a split second he then jumped sideways, toward my assistant, but stopped himself in midair before reaching her. Then, a split second later, he put himself right back where he'd started, let out a snort, lowered his head and acted as if nothing happened.

It all happened so quickly that I didn't have a chance to respond, and, in fact, just kept walking the entire time. In the span of less than a second, Mouse's worry gave him the opportunity to run into or over two different people, but instead he went out of his way to touch neither.

The more he began to trust this new, calmer way of going around people, the more opportunities he found to let go of anxiety. In fact, one warm sunny afternoon during a clinic in Florida, an auditor came to me while Mouse and I were waiting for the next rider to come into the arena. I was in the saddle and Mouse had taken the opportunity to take a quick nap in the sun, so I set the reins down on his neck. The auditor walked up and asked, "Where does he go?"

"Who," I asked.

"Him," she pointed at Mouse. "He's dead asleep. It'd take you forever to wake him up to get a job done."

With that, I reached down and with my index finger, lightly touched the rein draped over Mouse's neck. Mouse quietly opened his eyes and raised his head slightly, ready to go to work. I took my finger from the rein, Mouse hesitated a second, then lowered his head and went back to sleep. "He hasn't gone anywhere," I replied.

Mouse's transformation went beyond his work under saddle, though. When he'd first arrived, he'd been somewhat of a disruptive force in our herd, always on the move, randomly chasing others off the feed and stampeding the group anytime anybody went in the pasture to catch one of the other horses. But again, much of that behavior began to drop away after only a few months, and after about a year, he was often the first one to meet us at the gate in the morning.

He could still be wary of strangers from time to time, something he held on to until the day he died, and there were some people he never would warm up to. He made it very clear from the start that his trust could be earned, but it couldn't be taken, and people who knew him always seemed to feel a sense of accomplishment when Mouse let them approach and pet him.

That, like so many of his other traits, was simply part of who he was. They were things to be accepted and worked *with*, not things he needed to change so we could feel better about him or change so we could feel better about ourselves (as trainers). By simply giving him the time he needed, he'd been able to explain to us which of the behaviors he *could* feel better about, which ones we could negotiate on, and which ones were there to stay.

I think sometimes as horse people we have been so inundated with information on how to fix this problem or that problem that we think we have no other recourse but to attack any problem we come across head on, using any number of techniques or tools at our disposal. Then, if these things fail, or possibly even make the behavior worse, we simply go through the same protocol all over again, usually with the same unfortunate results.

I suppose it's part of the human condition: when something doesn't work, we want to fix it. If horses are troubled, we want to help them feel better. Of course, we are genuinely concerned about the horses, and we really do want them to feel better. But in some cases, we want them to feel better because their behavior is a direct reflection on us as horse people or trainers. If they aren't acting a certain way, then it somehow shows holes in our horse training/handling education, and we can't have that.

Looking at it perhaps another way, there is an interesting phenomenon a lot of martial artists go through when they first begin their training (particularly those who begin their training as adults). Usually after a month or two, new students begin to learn the basics of their chosen art. By this time, they have learned a few simple techniques like punches, grabs, kicks, or whatever, and because of this, some of these students begin to feel a sense of power in their newfound, although fledgling abilities.

What happens next is the interesting part. Many of these students, most of them peace-loving average people who never even considered getting into a scuffle with anybody before, suddenly begin to imagine sometimes elaborate self-defense scenarios. They may see themselves as the hero in a would-be mugging, or breaking up an attack from a bully out on the street somewhere, or any number of other scenarios in which they are able to use their newfound skills.

What is really happening is these students are learning a new skill, and they want to put it to use in some way—in *any* way. In fact, many are the new martial arts students who have only been training a short time and go out looking for a fight, only to have their hats handed to them by someone faster, bigger, and with more skills or talent.

I think, sometimes, as horse people, we are in the same boat. We go to this clinic or that one, learn a few skills, pick up a few new techniques, buy a flag or a rope or any number of other training tools, then suddenly feel the need to go out and find a situation in which to use them. Sometimes the situation is the right one, and we are able to make some significant progress and headway in helping a horse. Other times, the horse may appear to be complying, but isn't terribly willing, and still other times we have our hats handed to us by a horse that isn't buying into what we have to offer because what we are offering isn't what he needs.

If we're lucky, one day we learn the difference. If we don't, we will simply go along day after day, year after year, repeatedly making the same mistakes.

Not long ago an aikido master with forty years of experience was teaching a class I attended. At one point, he mentioned he learned almost all the technique he would ever need during the first ten years of his training. He then said he spent the next thirty years trying to figure out how *not* to use it.

It was a profound statement for me in both my martial arts training, as well as in my work with horses. Just because we might be good in martial arts doesn't mean that every argument we have with someone has to end with us punching them in the face. And just because we might be good at training horses doesn't mean that every horse we come across with some kind of issue needs us to train the problem out of them.

If there is one thing Mouse, and countless others like him, have taught me over the years, it's that the art in any art is in knowing when the skills we've worked so hard at refining are needed, and when they aren't. Of course, in the end, this is arguably the most difficult skill of all to develop, which in turn, also makes it the most valuable.

CHAPTER 6

Staying True

"We are all visitors to this time, this place. We are all just passing through. Our purpose here is to observe, to learn, to grow, to love…and then we return home."

A BORIGINAL P ROVERB

During a question-and-answer session at one of our recent clinics, an auditor asked if there were any current trainers or clinicians out there today that I admire or follow on a regular basis. I explained there were many horsemen and women I admire, but not many I follow.

The reason I haven't hitched my wagon to other trainers or clinicians is that I haven't really come across anybody (yet) in the horse world who really exemplifies an aspect of horsemanship (and life) that I not only feel is most important, but also of which I would like to gain better understanding.

Watching Walter work with a horse was like watching someone perform magic, especially for the young and impressionable boy I was back then. But even back then, and setting his amazing skills with horses aside, I realized there was an intangible quality to him that was not only very special, but that I just assumed was inherent in everybody who worked with horses.

He had a way about him that could put both animals and people at ease just by him being near—a quiet confidence, free of ego, that assured everything was going to be okay, even when it seemed as though maybe it wouldn't be—and a true kindness that seemed to permeate all he did and all he came in contact with. It really wasn't so much *what he did*, but *who he was*—and at least for me, that was the key. At the time, being with him on his little horse ranch had been my only experience with horses or horse people, so I didn't have anything to compare it to, so, as I said, I just assumed all horse people possessed the same qualities. I also knew they were qualities I didn't have, but again, I somehow just assumed if I stayed with horses long enough, I would develop them over time.

Unfortunately, as I grew older and moved into the "real world" of horses, I slowly began to realize that the particular qualities inherent in my old friend were not as common in others as I first thought or expected. In fact, I began seeing almost the complete opposite in many of the horse people I ran across. I watched people whose ego seemed to override their common sense, and who would routinely push horses much faster and harder than they were ready to go, almost always to the detriment of the horses. The more of this I saw, the more I began to realize in the "real" world, this kind of horse work appeared to be more the norm than the exception, and for a time I became quite discouraged over it.

Time passed, however, and as I began working various ranches and training for private individuals, I got away from actively looking for somebody with the same qualities as my old friend. I did, however, always keep my eyes and ears open *just in case* I happened to run across someone who might have them, and I continued to work with horses in a way that I believed honored what I learned from Walter all those years before.

Then, in the late 1980s, a friend and former employee at the dude ranch I managed invited me to a one-day demonstration to be given by a trainer he said worked with horses much the same way I did. I eagerly went, hoping my buddy may have found someone with those qualities I grew up with.

Before going any further, I do want to mention that nothing in what I am about to say is meant in a negative or derogatory way toward this trainer or his work. I don't know any of the reasons for the choices he made that day, or what may have been going on behind the scenes that influenced those decisions. Not only that, and speaking from experience, I know all too well how easy it is to have the best intentions while working with a horse only to have the whole thing go south before you know it. So, I want to be clear that this story is not told in judgment of the trainer or his skills.

The morning of the demo, the trainer was presented with a troubled five-year-old Morgan that had yet to be started. As the trainer went into the round pen with the horse, his demeanor and temperament toward the horse seemed very much like Walter's, and as he began his work with the horse, it was as if I stepped back in time to that little horse ranch of my childhood. I watched and listened intently as the trainer eased his way around the Morgan, and throughout the morning the little horse transformed from being wide-eyed and terrified of everything and everybody, to being as quiet as a church mouse, attentively following the trainer's every move and request.

By the time we broke for lunch, I was convinced I was watching someone who lived what he taught, and I couldn't wait to see what he might do with a different horse after lunch. Of course, that was assuming that having gotten the Morgan to such a great place that morning, he was finished with the little gelding.

I was a bit surprised, and a little confused that afternoon when I saw the Morgan still in the round pen. I was even more confused when the trainer began talking about the horse having trouble with "respect" (something he hadn't even mentioned during the morning session) and then a bit shocked when he hurried the little horse through a first-time saddling, which the gelding didn't take well.

The trainer no sooner tightened his cinch than the gelding exploded, bucking, bawling, and crashing into the panels of the pen. The trainer kept the gelding moving forward by tossing the end of a lariat at him and, eventually, the gelding lined out, and after a time, stopped, sides heaving and drenched in sweat.

The trainer then got on the young horse and the whole thing started all over again with the horse bucking, bolting, bawling, and crashing into the fence. To his credit, the trainer was able to stay with the Morgan the entire time, eventually riding him into a state of exhaustion. He did do some very nice work with the horse after all of that, and the truth is, I did pick up some new ideas throughout the day. But for me, that was all it was, just more technique and not at all what I originally hoped to see or feel.

Over the next several years I would hear about other trainers and clinicians who sounded as if they had the qualities I'd seen in my old friend, but each time I went to see them or watch one of their videos or talk to them in person, I knew almost right away that it wasn't the case. (As a side note here, it was also during this time when I heard about Tom Dorrance for the first time, who I am certain possessed the qualities I experienced growing up. But unfortunately, I never had the honor of meeting or watching him in person.)

Now again, while I most certainly appreciated, respected, and admired many of these trainers, as well as their skills and what they were able to accomplish with a horse, and while there was always something to be learned from each one of them, the simple truth is that none that I met were teaching what I really wanted to learn. Maybe a better way to say that is they weren't *living* what I wanted to learn. And for me, that was the important part.

I knew what I was looking for could not be turned on when it was convenient and turned off when it was not. It seemed to either be part of who the person was, or it wasn't. To that end, I watched over and over as trainers and clinicians would take all the time in the world to help a horse, and then often treat the owner like a red-headed stepchild. To me, that way of going is at the heart of the incongruence I'm trying to avoid.

A number of trainers and clinicians out there often tell their students that they are there for the horse, not the rider. That kind of statement alone gives me enough pause not to want to spend too much time following those trainers. As I see it, the horse and rider should be a unit. Seems to me splitting them by the way they are treated or taught, by its very nature, creates a disconnect that can be difficult for riders to overcome, and creating a disconnect is not the kind of thing I want to pass along to folks I work with.

Obviously, there are as many teaching and learning styles out there as there are teachers and students. However, in general, most teachers, regardless of the subject, not only teach what they know, but also teach how *they've* been taught. If their teachers imparted information with a general lack of regard for the students, then the students will often teach the same way. If they've been taught with respect and dignity, they will often offer the same to their students. I was taught with the latter and having experienced it at such a young age it was one thing that ended up leaving an indelible mark on me that even after all these years will not run or fade. To that end, I not only understand what it is I'm looking for in a teacher, but I also know and understand what I'm *not* looking for.

I did eventually find the teachers I was searching for, men and women who didn't just teach what they knew but lived what they taught. These were individuals whose main goal wasn't to prove how superior their own skills were, but rather to help their students progress in the skills they were working so hard at improving, and whose kindness and empathy for others transcended the classroom.

But it wasn't in the horse world I found these teachers. Rather, I found them in the world of martial arts. And I would come to understand these particular teachers had two main things in common: They all chose *their* teachers wisely, and none allowed outside influences to distract them from moving in the direction they felt was right for them.

One of these teachers in particular, Hiroshi Ikeda Sensei, an aikido master and one of the kindest men I have ever met, ultimately made such an impression on me that I would not only study and train with him every chance I had, but I found myself talking about him quite often in both our horsemanship clinics as well as in our *aibado* (aikido for horsemen) workshops. In fact, I was in England some time back and had an opportunity to talk with a friend and fellow student of aikido who'd been able to take a weekend seminar from Ikeda Sensei on one of his trips to the United Kingdom.

When I asked my friend about his experience, he expressed how impressed he was with Sensei not just as an instructor, but also in how kind and generous in all aspects he was to everybody, every day, regardless of rank or experience level. He then said something that really summed up what not only kept me searching for teachers like Ikeda Sensei, but also what drew me to Walter all those years ago. He said the difference for him was that when you were with Sensei, when you were in the *dojo* with him, or listening to him as he explained a technique, or most certainly if you touched him, you could immediately feel his *humanity*.

And there it was. After all these years, the thing I've been searching for in both my teachers and in my own work with horses finally had a name—*humanity*.

I guess the reason it has been so difficult for me to define what I've been searching for is because this thing, this *humanity*, can't be forced, or faked, or mechanically replicated. It has to be felt, experienced, practiced and worked at over and over, day in and day out, until finally it just becomes part of who we are and is in everything we do—not just in what we do with horses.

Speaking for myself there've been times—days, weeks, and even months—where I have missed the mark on a monumental scale, both with horses and in my life. Apologies have had to be made and lessons were learned. And then the work goes on.

Several years ago, I experienced what I felt was a major breakthrough in my horsemanship. The interesting thing was I wasn't anywhere near a horse when it happened.

I was invited to dinner after aikido class one evening by Ikeda Sensei. It was a great honor to have been invited, and even though it was already after nine at night and I still had nearly an hour to drive to get home, I gratefully accepted. Three of us—Sensei, another student who had also been invited, and I—drove to a nearby restaurant where we sat down at a table and ordered our meals.

We engaged in small talk for a few minutes before Sensei asked what I did for a living. "I work with horses," I told him. "It's why I began studying aikido. I wanted to find something to help me improve my work."

He smiled, folded his arms over his chest and leaned back in his chair. "Has it?" It was clear by the expression on his face he already knew the answer. "It has." I smiled. "Very much." He nodded.

He then asked what the similarities were between horsemanship and aikido, and for the next few minutes I shared with him and the other student at the table what I had found so far. I also told him my ultimate goal with horses was to find a way to communicate with them on the same level they communicated with one another—a level so subtle it is often difficult, if not impossible to see.

"I know nothing of horse," Sensei said, placing his hand flat on the table between us. "But maybe this how *they* do." He asked me to place my hand on his and then push down so that he would be unable to lift his hand from the table. I did. He tried to lift his hand, but I was holding it down with as much pressure and energy as I could, and his hand wouldn't budge. "For example, this how *we* do," he said, motioning for me to continue holding his hand down. "We fight, go against partner."

Then, without warning, I felt my body begin to change. The change, an uncontrollable relaxation of all my tense muscles, began in the hand that I was using to hold his hand to the table, but very quickly passed all the way through me all the way to my feet. Then, from somewhere deep inside him, what I can only describe as a slow wave began to build. He smiled again.

"This how *they* do?" It was more of a question than a statement. "Unity first. Then go together." His hand, with mine on top, and me trying in vain to keep his from moving, lifted effortlessly from the table.

"Change outside by change inside first." He took his hand from the table, crossed his arms over his chest, and leaned back in his chair again. "In aikido, unity difficult to see. Feel for unity inside self and partner, make more easy."

The idea of developing a change in ourselves from the inside in order to help change or soften a partner in aikido was not new to me. In fact, the class Sensei just finished teaching, as well as a number of the classes he taught and which I attended, was entirely on the internal elements of aikido. I even found a great deal of success using the same principles when dealing with difficult horses since I began studying with him.

However, he said something this time that really caught my attention. He said unity was difficult to see, but if one feels for unity in both oneself and one's partner, it can make it easier. Was he saying that "internal" unity could actually be seen? If so, would that be the key to being able to somehow physically see the kind of subtle communication horses offer each other? The kind of communication that seems invisible to us?

As I continued to attend Sensei's classes, I tried to pay very close attention, even closer than I'd been, to what he offered his partners, and if I could see any kind of minute visible change in them prior to him making contact with them. I found there were times when a change was visible, but to be honest, no more than I would normally see in a similar situation.

Then, during one class, I saw it. Well, actually, I think we all saw it. In fact, a blind man could have seen it. Sensei asked a student to be his partner during a demonstration. The partner was to take a hold of Sensei's wrist so Sensei could demonstrate unity through contact. And that's when it happened.

Just as the partner (Uke) went to reach for Sensei's wrist in a very powerful way, a little smile crossed Sensei's face. As the smile appeared, and before the two made contact, there was an ever-so-slight dissipation of Uke's intensity. A quiet but unified "Ooh" rippled through all of us watching, then, upon actually making contact with Sensei's wrist, the student collapsed uncontrollably to the mat.

"Unity inside first, then inside partner," Sensei said. "See unity?"
We all nodded, having witnessed the obvious connection between the two before contact was made. Sensei motioned for Uke to try again. The student again reached for Sensei's wrist in a powerful way. Sensei again smiled, but Uke didn't seem to lose any intensity in his reach. Still, when he made contact, Uke again crumpled to the mat. Sensei turned to us, still smiling.

"See unity?" We all sat quietly, none of us having actually seen the point of relaxation in Uke that we saw previously. "In aikido, unity difficult to see. Feel for unity in self and partner, make more easy."

It was then that the point I believe he was trying to make struck me. We have a tendency to look for outside physical changes, but seldom look for changes on the inside. Yet it is the internal changes that lead to the external changes—in both us and our partners.

It's very much the same in horsemanship. We are taught to watch or feel for external changes in the horses we work with but pay little attention to the internal changes. Even when we do look for internal changes in the horse, we often are paying little attention to what is going on inside us.

I continue to attend as many of Sensei's classes on the internal elements of aikido as possible, and, not surprisingly, I've found that the concepts I learn from him can be directly applied to horses in almost any situation. I have also been able to improve my own internal awareness, which is in no way at the level in which Sensei operates, but still light years better than it was before I began studying with him.

One of the things I also noticed as my own internal awareness began to improve is that my ability to see and feel internal changes in horses has not only improved, but it has gotten more accurate as well. Whereas in the past I might have waited for some tiny external change to occur before I would pick up on what the horse might be thinking or feeling, now I could sort of "feel" what was going to happen before the external change in the horse would actually show up. These changes in awareness translated directly into the level of softness, or feel, that my body was able to produce and replicate. So much so, in fact, that just five years ago I was completely unaware that such a level of softness even existed in me or in horses. This change was like suddenly being able to see in three dimensions after a lifetime of only being able to see in two.

Of course, when any major shift in skill or understanding of concepts begins to take hold, the mind and body have a period of adjustment, or recalibration, if you will. It's a part of growth that can be pretty uncomfortable at times. And it was no different for me. As I tried to navigate between what I had always known and done and this new understanding, I found myself floundering a bit, making mistakes I didn't usually make, struggling with my feel and timing and even questioning the direction I was going. It was very unsettling, to say the least.

But as time went on, I decided to just accept what was going on instead of fighting or worrying about it, and soon after that, things began to smooth out. Eventually, the fog of uncertainty lifted, as it always does, and the path became clearer and a bit easier to navigate. Now, several years later, I find this new direction not only very exciting, but also endless in its possibilities.

Five years ago, I could not have imagined the level of softness that would be available to me today. Today, I can't imagine what will be available in the years to come. But one thing is certain, I am sure looking forward to the journey.

WHY DO HORSES DO WHAT THEY DO?

CHAPTER 7

The Horse's Perspective

"Pride is concerned with who is right.
Humility is concerned with what is right."
EZRA TAFT BENSON

I t was a little after ten in the morning and already proving to be one of those days where the heat in the air was shimmering a few feet above the open fields and the gravel road in the distance. I'd just dumped out and cleaned, and was refilling the water tank to the south pasture when Walter walked through the gate and turned loose a little gelding named Mack whose feet he'd just trimmed. About that same time, three or four horses from the herd made their way over to get a drink from the rapidly filling metal tank.

Walter slipped the leather halter from Mack's nose, glanced at the approaching horses and went back through the gate, closing and latching it behind him. Mack stood about where he'd been left, the heat of the day causing him to look a little like a once inflated balloon that lost half its air.

Having finally reached the tank, the horses lowered their heads and just started to drink when the previously half-inflated Mack seemed to suddenly grow about three feet. His ears flattened, he rocked back on his haunches and launched himself toward the horses at the tank.

A brief but animated kerfuffle ensued as the horses, seemingly as surprised as I was at the unexpected turn of events, crashed into one another, trying to escape the little gelding's wrath. Having quickly gotten themselves organized, they wheeled and jumped as one in the opposite direction of Mack's line of attack.

As they stampeded away, one of them, a paint mare named Misty, snapped her tail and gave a kick in Mack's direction with both hind feet. Mack slid to a stop in front of the tank, his back end almost touching the ground, his nose pointed straight up in the air, easily escaping contact from the kick.

The whole thing took less than a couple seconds, and still, with me being just on the other side of the fence and only a couple feet away from the activity, I found myself instinctively recoiling, while at the same time glancing at Walter. He was finishing up latching the gate, halter, and rope in the crook of his arm, looking as if nothing at all out of the ordinary happened.

The horses cantered away while Mack, apparently satisfied with the outcome, let the air out of the balloon, lowered his head and closed his eyes as if the heat of the day was just too oppressive for him to do anything else. To my surprise, having thought he ran the other horses off so he could drink, Mack didn't give the water tank so much as a sideways look.

Walter came over and glanced at the near-full water tank.

"Gonna be hot enough to complain about today," he said, taking the half-smoked cigarette between his fingers and letting bluish smoke roll from the corner of his mouth. "Keep an eye on all the waters."

He turned to walk away.

"Why'd Mack do that?" I asked.

"Do what?" He stopped, glancing over his shoulder.

"He chased those horses off and didn't even get a drink!"

"He's a horse," he took another drag. "Sometimes they do that."

It wasn't the first time I'd heard that answer, nor would it be the last. In fact, I'm not sure how many times I saw a horse do something that I didn't understand, asked

Walter about it, and got the same or some similar type of answer. "Just a horse being a horse." "Can't figure horses sometimes." "Seems strange, don't it?"

Back then I took Walter's answers to mean he didn't know why horses offer up what I perceived as odd or unpredictable behavior. But now I realize what he was probably saying, in his own way, was horses will always act like horses. Their motivations for doing things are different than ours. As a result, behavior that might seem strange or unreasonable to us, being that we only see the world through the lens of being human, would be perfectly reasonable to a horse because they see the world through the lens of being a horse. And those are two completely different lenses.

I also believe Walter answered the way he did because he accepted horses for who and what they were. He saw horses as horses without the need to run them through any other lens just so it would be easier for him to understand them. Because of that, he could accept their behavior for what it was... *just horses being horses.*

So, when he would say something like, "Can't figure horses sometimes," or "Seems strange, don't it?" he meant it in the literal sense. Horses *can* be hard to figure sometimes, and horse behavior *does* seem strange to *us*—because we're not horses.

Without a lot of emphasis put on *why* horses did what they did, what I was left with was just the behavior itself and trying to figure out ways to deal with it when necessary. So, as I progressed in my learning, that was where my focus went, dealing with behavior rather than worrying so much about where it was coming from.

It wasn't until years later that that way of thinking shifted for me. I'd been going to see a little gelding at a boarding facility near Denver once a week for a couple months. He was a friendly little bulldog-built Quarter Horse that was great to be around on the ground, but not much fun to ride due to persistent behavioral issues. It was not uncommon for him to crowhop, bolt, refuse to move, turn, stop, or back up, all in one session. Each time I went to see him we would seem to achieve some semblance of success in getting him to feel better, but then within a day or two all the behaviors would come back. It was about that same time a young equine chiropractor had been showing up and working on some of the other horses at the facility, and I noticed the horses he worked on always seemed to go better after his sessions with them.

After watching the chiropractor work and listening to him explain what he was doing, I asked if he would take a look at the Quarter Horse gelding. To make a long story short, after just one session with him, most of the behavioral issues I'd been trying to help this horse resolve for the past two months seemed to go away. Three sessions later, the behaviors were completely gone.

That was when I realized while some behaviors horses offer up certainly fit into the "horse being a horse" category, other behaviors, like the ones the little bulldog gelding had been struggling with, may very well be coming from some other source. Having come to that realization, I knew I needed to figure out and understand the difference.

Little did I know at the time that making that one decision would send me on a decades-long journey of discovery about horses that would allow me to learn from some of the world leaders in hoof care, saddle fit, chiropractic, dental care, acupressure and acupuncture, cold lasers, bodywork (after which I became a trained bodyworker), nutrition, ophthalmology, and neurology/brain science.

———

The great martial artist Bruce Lee once said, *"Before I learned the art, a punch was just a punch, and a kick, just a kick. After I learned the art, a punch was no longer a punch, a kick, no longer a kick. Now that I understand the art, a punch is just a punch, and a kick is just a kick."*

He would explain how as he progressed in his training, he sought out the help of masters to help him understand the nuances of a punch and kick, and he learned how to break down each individual component of both. He learned different ways of striking and kicking, and how many times to use each, given any variety of situations. He studied and practiced and studied and practiced some more, so much so that eventually he was no longer able to process the information he was taking in effectively and efficiently. At that point, he said, *"A punch was no longer a punch, a kick no longer a kick."*

At some point, things began to shift. His control, focus, timing, and power all began to improve to where he no longer had to think about which punch or kick to execute, when to use them, or how much energy to use. His speed and timing improved as did his balance and precision. Eventually, and after many years, he reached the point where he no longer needed to think about technique or mechanics because both were now second nature. *"Once again, a punch was just a punch, and a kick was just a kick."*

Something similar happened to me when it comes to understanding horse behavior. Early on I believed horse behavior to be just horse behavior. It was the way horses behaved in relation to how they felt. Then, as I began to study the different aspects and potential causes and effects of behavior, horse behavior no longer seemed just horse behavior anymore.

When I was learning about chiropractic, all unwanted behavior seemed to stem from chiropractic issues. When I was learning about saddle fit, I started to see unwanted behavior as potential saddle-fit issues. It was the same when it came to teeth, bodywork, nutrition, and all the rest.

Then, over years of studying and observation, things began to shift again. I started to see that while there's no question a lot of unwanted behavior can be traced back to some underlying physical or emotional issue, in the end, the behavior is just behavior. It's the way a horse acts in relation to how the horse feels.

Today when I work with a horse and rider, and almost always before we even get started, I look to see if there are any glaring physical issues or asymmetries in the horse's movement. I look for any possible signs of saddle fit, dental, or feet issues. Depending on the horse and the behavior exhibited, I might ask what the horse is being fed, what the living situation is, or even how the horse is bred (something I'll discuss in more detail later—see p. 123). I'm never looking for anything specific with any of this, nor am I making any judgments about what I see. Rather, I try to just take the information in and put it in the back of my mind. If the horse shows some kind of behavior, it is usually associated with one or more of the possible causes I've already noticed, and then I discuss it with the rider.

Much of the time, we can figure out the possible cause of an unwanted behavior just by the rider describing the behavior and then watching the horse go. An example of this happened several years ago when one of our clinic hosts, an accomplished trainer and rider, asked me to take a look at a horse she had been riding for a client.

She'd been experiencing a couple issues with the little mare she couldn't quite put her finger on. The first was that they would often be going around nicely, then suddenly the mare would put her head almost to the ground for several strides before throwing her head almost straight up and shaking it. After the head shake, she would then put her head in a normal position. This behavior usually got worse the faster the horse went.

The other issue she was having was that the mare was stumbling, which also got worse the faster she went. The stumbling had gotten so bad that they had actually fallen once while at the canter.

Stumbling can show up when a horse's feet have grown too long or from physical issues or a tightness somewhere in the body, such as the shoulders, withers, and neck. We've also seen it in horses with substantial dental issues. But this horse didn't appear to have any of these issues.

It wasn't long after the pair started cantering an eighty-foot circle in the arena that both issues the clinic host described became apparent. Within a few strides after their transition to the canter, the mare dropped her head so low her nose nearly touched the ground. She then tipped her head from side to side, lifted it so her nose almost pointed toward the sky, shook it again, then lowered it to a normal position.

About a half lap later she repeated almost the exact same behavior, something she would do numerous times over the next several minutes and regardless of the direction in which she was ridden. She also stumbled a couple times as well, although she always caught herself.

Nothing about the behaviors the mare was offering looked normal to me. Horses that lower their head while ridden might do so as a way to stretch, but they seldom tip their head from side to side while their nose is almost on the ground, and almost never follow it with sticking their nose straight up in the air and shaking their head. As far as stumbling, that is certainly not uncommon. However, what was uncommon was that when I asked the host if she'd ever seen the horse stumble while cantering around out in the pasture, her answer was yes. Not only that, but she said the mare did all the behaviors without a rider on her back, including everything she did with her head.

This was an important bit of information. Generally speaking, if horses exhibit some sort of odd or unwanted behavior under saddle, but not when they are out on their own, then the behavior is likely caused by something associated with their rider, such as training or ill-fitting tack, or possibly even something physical that only shows up when they have weight on their back. If, on the other hand, the same behavior shows up whether the horse is being ridden or not, that could very well be a sign that whatever the issue is, it's there all the time and might not have anything to do with the rider.

At face value, the mare's behaviors weren't necessarily out of the ordinary as far as things that horses do from time to time. But they didn't seem quite right, either. The problem, at least initially, was that I couldn't put my finger on what was going on. Over the years I had seen variations of everything the mare was offering, but never all of them together, and never as dramatic as what she was presenting.

As I watched her head drop to the ground for about the tenth time, followed by the raised head shaking, I started getting the impression the mare might be having trouble with her vision. I wasn't convinced this was the case. Over the years I'd seen quite a few horses with odd behavior that had me wondering if they were having trouble with their vision. Out of those, only a handful ended up being diagnosed as such.

But still, this looked pretty strange. I filmed the mare's behavior and sent it off to a friend who happens to be a leading equine ophthalmologist to get his opinion. He suggested taking close-up photos of each of her eyes after dark, using a flash. If anything was getting in the way of her vision, it would probably show up in the photos.

Sure enough, the photos showed what looked like a small, jagged-edged island, partially covering the lens in her right eye. I sent the photos to my friend, who confirmed that what we were seeing was a floating cyst. Because the cyst was floating, she was able to move it around by raising, lowering, and shaking her head. As it turned out, her stumbling was a result of her vision being impaired and everything else was nothing more than her trying to move the cyst so she could see better.

Luckily, this was able to be resolved through a non-invasive procedure by a local equine ophthalmologist and the mare was able to go back to her normal activity within a relatively short time after having it done.

———

Not long ago I had an interesting situation come up regarding horse behavior. In this case, the behavior itself was relatively innocuous and not really an issue. However, the owner's understanding about the behavior, and its perceived cause, became so troubling for her that she was considering getting out of horses altogether.

It was lunch time, but Mary was already standing in the middle of the large indoor arena when I came in to get ready for the afternoon sessions of the clinic. Her horse, a nondescript chestnut gelding named Sharpie, was unsaddled and standing quietly by her side, head down, half asleep.

Sharpie, I would learn, was Mary's first horse. Riding and owning horses had been a lifelong dream for her and her husband, which they finally realized when their kids moved out and started lives of their own. They bought some horse property, both started taking lessons, and then eventually bought Sharpie, the horse she'd been leasing from her instructor.

"Hi there," I said. "You two up next?"

"Yes," she replied.

I went over to my PA system, replaced the batteries in the transmitter of my wireless mic, and turned back to Mary.

"He looks like a pretty nice guy." I smiled.

Mary didn't reply. She turned to Sharpie with a pained half-smile and gave him a light pat on the neck.

It was the first day of the clinic, and it was often the case that new riders (that is, riders I haven't seen or worked with before) often came in a little on the nervous side. I'd seen it many times before. In fact, there was a time years ago when I had two riders at back-to-back clinics who were so nervous they literally got sick just before coming in the pen to work.

So, I knew nervousness when I saw it. Mary didn't look nervous. She looked sad.

"Everything okay?" I asked.

"I'm hoping you can help us with our relationship." She didn't look away from her horse.

I headed over to where they stood but stopped well short. Sharpie looked up and turned an ear in my direction, but that was about it as far as his interest in me.

"Relationship?"

"He doesn't trust me." It was very matter of fact as if it were a foregone conclusion, even though the picture of the two of them standing there certainly didn't look like a horse-owner pair where trust was an issue.

"Mind if I ask why you feel that way?"

There was a long pause before Mary finally turned toward me, hand still on her gelding's neck.

"Can I show you?"

"Of course."

She turned to Sharpie, patted him, draped the halter rope over his neck and re-moved his halter. They stood together looking no different than when he'd been wearing the halter a few seconds earlier. After about a minute, she gently raised the halter to his nose. Sharpie turned away from her slightly. She lowered the halter and looked at me.

"See what I mean?"

"I'm not sure I do," I said, a little perplexed.

Mary explained she'd read an article in which the author stated a horse turning away from you when you offered a halter or bridle was a sure sign your horse had a problem with you. As Mary described it, the turning away was the horse telling you they didn't trust you, and by the time the horse was showing this kind of behavior, a great deal of harm had already been done to the relationship between you.

So far, Mary hadn't found a way to help her horse be okay with being haltered or bridled without him turning away, and because this article was written by someone she admired and who's opinion she trusted, she was now questioning her fledgling skills *and* the relationship between her and Sharpie.

As can often be the case in situations like this, the more she thought about the whole thing, the worse she felt. Not wanting to be a constant source of worry for Sharpie, Mary was now considering finding him a home with someone he would feel more comfortable with.

I suppose to some folks, Mary's response to the situation might seem like an overreaction. It's not. This kind of thing happens with horse folks all the time, both to those with experience as well as those without. Horse people trying to improve their own knowledge and skills routinely put their trust in the opinions of established trainers, instructors, and professionals. But for the relatively inex-perienced, one of these trusted professionals telling them they are damaging their relationship with their horse can really be devastating, even, as was the case with Mary, when it's not true.

I explained to Mary that while a horse turning away when we introduce the hal-ter or bridle *can* be a sign of a relationship problem, more times than not, it isn't the case. Horses turn away from a halter for numerous reasons, the majority of which simply boil down to misunderstandings that have become learned behavior.

Horses who have settled into learned behavior that doesn't cause them much stress, whether that behavior was taught intentionally or unintentionally, usually have some level of comfort while performing that behavior. After all, if they believe the response they offer is what we want, then there's no reason for them to be upset when offering the response.

Taking that a step further, if they aren't upset offering the response, then they probably aren't looking at what's going on between us as a deal-breaker in our relationship. That's what seemed to be going on between Mary and Sharpie.

I asked her to offer him the halter again, which she did. Again, Sharpie turned away slightly as she brought it toward his nose, and again she lowered the halter and looked at me. I asked if what she'd just done was what she always did. Specifically, did she always lower the halter after he turned away? She said she did. I explained he was probably seeing her removing the halter as a reward for him turning his head. I asked her to try again.

She brought the halter toward his nose and as if on cue, he turned his head. This time, however, I asked her to keep the halter right where it was when he turned his head, which she did. We waited only about five seconds before Sharpie slowly brought his head back, his nose stopping directly above the halter. Mary gently lifted the halter and at the same time Sharpie lowered his nose. The halter went on without an issue and Sharpie's relaxed expression never changed.

We repeated this whole thing several more times over the next five minutes or so. By the end, not only was Sharpie no longer turning away, but he would willingly offer to lower his nose into the open halter. His doing so brought a noticeable smile to Mary's face.

I'd like to take a minute here and reiterate that horse behavior is just horse behavior. It's what horses do to communicate how they feel. Trying to understand possible underlying causes of behavior, especially when it's unwanted, is certainly a good thing. Making up stories about the behavior or insisting on placing blame or fault for the behavior is not.

As I mentioned earlier, when I was with Walter and in the years that followed, I learned to deal with behavior at face value. I didn't give the *why* much thought and because most of my work was solitary, I hardly ever had anybody ask me *why*. It wasn't until I started working for the public that the question began coming up, and as the "professional" I was expected to have an answer. Not only did people want to know *why* a horse was behaving the way they were, but quite often they also wanted to know what the horse was *thinking* any time they offered the behavior.

I'm going to let you in on a little secret. Nobody really knows what a horse is thinking. I suppose there are some folks who would argue that animal communicators know what horses think. Maybe they do. But because my experience with animal communicators over the years has been a mixed bag (some good, some not so much) I'm going to respectfully exclude them from this conversation.

What you're usually getting when someone (myself included) offers an opinion about what a horse is thinking is an educated guess based on years of experience and observation. Here's the thing, when you spend hundreds of thousands of hours working with and riding countless numbers of horses, it only makes sense that at some point you'll start picking up on reliable patterns of behavior given similar situations.

It's not long before these behavior patterns become so familiar that it's easy to predict what the horse might do next once a certain pattern is observed. As a result, the person making the prediction appears to know what the horse is thinking when they really don't.

Probably the most common and most recognizable behavior pattern is a horse that "bloats" because of being girthed too tight. I've seen horses all over the world who have figured out this particular behavior as a way to save themselves from being uncomfortable. I suspect all of them fell into the pattern in much the same way. Still, I doubt anybody really knows what they were *thinking* when they figured it out. We assume they somehow put two and two together—bloating now + releasing later = comfort. But that's how we humans, using our great big human brains, would work it out. Horses don't have a human brain, so it would be difficult, if not impossible for them to decipher even that simple equation.

More likely what happened was the horse just stumbled on the solution due to defending themselves from constant careless hands. If I had to guess, after, say, three

times of a girth being pulled quick and hard, the fourth time the horse instinctively tensed or expanded the muscles in the area under the girth (much like we would,
knowing someone was going to jab us in the ribs) as a way to protect themselves. The
horse's behavior was more of an instinctive response than anything else, but the horse
finds the girthing process isn't as uncomfortable when they do it. So, the next time
someone girths the horse up, they repeat the thing that benefitted them the last time.
Just like that, a pattern of behavior has been created in the horse, and they more than
likely never gave it much, if any, thought while it was happening.

I bring up this idea of people believing they know what a horse is thinking because
I've seen the kinds of problems doing so can create. In fact, I've watched folks who
were so concerned about their horses' thoughts that they became all but paralyzed
when working with them. One situation a while back comes to mind.

The clinic was in a medium-sized covered arena with three open sides. The short
wall to the south had a view of the parking lot. Just inside the arena on that wall was
the check-in table and the auditors. The north short wall had a view of the woods that
grew about thirty feet just outside the arena. The east long wall opened to rolling hills
and pasture, and the other was lined with stalls, all of which opened into the arena.

I was answering questions from the auditors when the next rider, a fellow named
Wayne, rode in on a big bay gelding. I watched him ride along the wall lined with
stalls, past the short wall with the view of the woods, and then back toward where I
sat on my horse, finishing up the questions with the auditors.

The gelding seemed a little nervous, but not bad—meaning, he was checking out
the surroundings, but not calling, spooking, jigging, or offering up any of the other
worry-induced behaviors a horse in a new environment might offer.

About the time I finished with the last question, Wayne rode up, having completed two full laps around the arena. Wayne introduced himself and his horse, whose
name was Marty. He'd owned Marty for about a year and a half, having bought him
at a ranch horse sale. Apparently, the big bay came from a working ranch somewhere
in West Texas, and pretty much had "been there and done that." Wayne went on to
say they mostly trail rode, did a little cattle work, and attended horsemanship clinics
when the opportunity arose.

"What can I help you with?" I asked.

"I want his thought to stay with me," he replied.

Over the years a lot of riders had told me they wanted their horse's *attention* on them, but I couldn't recall anybody ever saying they wanted their horse's *thought* on them. I wasn't exactly sure how to take what he'd said and wondered if he misspoke and meant he wanted Marty's attention. I say this because my understanding is that attention and thought are two separate things, with one ultimately being a consequence of the other.

For me, attention is *external* in nature. Something in the environment attracts a horse's interest or heightens their awareness. Thought, on the other hand, is *internal* in nature. An opinion formed in the horse's mind, regarding the thing that caught their attention. For example, a horse hears a noise and turns toward it (attention). The horse sees the noise is caused by a person carrying a bucket and concludes the noise is not a threat (thought). The horse doesn't have a lot of control over the former as the reaction is driven by instinct. With the latter, however, the horse has processed the information through past experiences and come to what we might refer to as an "informed decision" as to what to do about it.

"Do you mean, his attention?" I asked. "You want his attention on you?"

'No," he responded. "I want his thought on me. It's all over the place right now, especially down on the other end." He motioned toward the far end of the arena, the short wall near the woods.

"Mind showing me?"

"Yeah, okay." He turned the bay and started for the other end of the arena, staying relatively close to the long wall lined with stalls. I followed close behind on my horse, Rocky.

As we got near the far end and made the turn from the long wall to the short wall, Marty looked out toward the woods.

"See what I mean?" Wayne said, a hint of agitation in his voice. "His thought is all the way out there somewhere instead of on me." He paused for a second, then added, "Look how worried he is."

The gelding didn't look all that worried to me. In fact, I didn't think he look worried at all. He didn't raise his head, he didn't tighten his body, his breathing hadn't changed, he didn't speed up or slow down, his eyes didn't widen, and he didn't even come close to offering to spook or shy. As he passed the middle of the short wall, Marty's head came back to a neutral position, his ears and eyes relaxed.

I was just getting ready to mention to Wayne that I thought Marty looked fine when they turned the corner from the short wall to the east long wall. A small group of horses grazed in one of the nearby pastures just outside the arena and Marty turned to have a look, his quiet demeanor never changing.

"See?" Wayne sounded mildly exasperated. "Every time his thought leaves me, he starts to worry."

Again, I didn't see it.

After watching the horses for a few steps, Marty turned his head back inside the arena and continued. A horse called from inside the barn and Marty looked briefly in that direction but didn't call back or change his demeanor.

"Now his thought is over there!"

By this time, the pair were heading back toward the auditors, one of whom got up to move her chair into the sun streaming in from the east. Marty turned his attention to her.

"See what I mean?" Wayne blurted. "His thought is everywhere except on me!"

"Okay," I said. "I understand what you're saying. But maybe we can look at it a little differently. How about this? What would you like to be doing with him right now?"

"I want his thought on me," Wayne's voice was raised slightly.

"I understand that. But just for argument's sake, let's say his thought *is* on you. What would you want to do then?"

"But it's not!"

"Let's say it is. What would you want to be working on with him? Lateral work? Transitions? Turns? Stops?"

"I don't know." There was anger in his voice. "Probably transitions."

"Okay," I shrugged. "What's going on with your transitions? Are they too fast? Too slow? Too...."

"They're too slow, because his thought is never on me!"

I'd like to stop here for a minute and explain a few things that we were able to cover with Wayne that eventually helped him see things a little differently between him and Marty.

The first two things I'd like to mention may seem completely unrelated to this situation, but if you bear with me, you'll see how they connect.

As a student advances through the ranks in aikido, eventually the student will have developed enough skills, knowledge, and technique to be introduced to an exercise called *randori*. Randori is where the student is asked to fend off multiple attackers at once. The number of attackers can range anywhere from two or three upward to ten or twelve.

The first few times the student is faced with more than one training partner, they are almost always overwhelmed by the attacks within a matter of seconds. The reason for this is the student new to randori will see the first attack coming, try to figure out what kind of attack it will be, then mentally run through the long list of techniques they know trying to choose the right one. The precious few seconds it takes for them to decide on a technique causes their timing to be slightly off, although usually still good enough to defend against that first attacker.

No sooner has the student taken care of the first attacker then a second is already on the way. The student once again tries to figure out what kind of attack is coming and mentally runs through the list of techniques. This uses up more time and adds to the delay in the performance of the student's technique. Because the delay in the student's timing has again increased, the second attacker becomes a little more difficult to deal with than the first, and that takes up even more time.

Then, while the student is still dealing with the second attacker, a third is now on the way. Usually, by the time the third or fourth attacker moves in, the student is already overwhelmed and no longer able to defend themselves due to the ever-increasing delay in timing caused by trying to think their way through each individual situation.

Most of the time, in preparation for randori, the student's instructor has spent time encouraging them to respond in the moment when presented with multiple attackers. The student is encouraged to stay out of their head and let their body do what it has been trained to do, void of thought.

The reason for this, as the student finds out, is that in fast-moving situations such as randori, the more we try to think or reason our way through it, the further behind we get. Soon, we're so far behind, the situation begins to control us instead of us controlling the situation.

This kind of thing is extremely common in horsemanship and shows up in many forms. In Wayne's case, however, he was so concerned about where his horse's thought was that he completely lost track of the reality of what was going on. In fact, he talked himself into believing Marty was worried when he wasn't, and the cause for Marty's sluggish transitions was because Marty refused to keep his thought on Wayne, which also wasn't true. But more about that in a minute.

The second thing I covered with Wayne works in conjunction with the first and has to do with self-control. Ours, not the horse. For this, I'll use another martial arts analogy.

We begin each of our *aibado* (aikido for horsemen) classes with a simple movement drill. The exercise begins with students standing with their right foot forward, left foot back, much as one might do if you took a step and then stopped. From this stance, the student takes a step so that the left foot is then forward, the right is back.

Then, instead of taking another step, the students turn around, sweeping the right leg behind them so that they are facing the opposite direction, still with their left leg forward, right leg back. To complete the movement, the students step with their right foot, sweep with their left and end up back where they started, facing the original direction, right foot forward, left leg back.

The movement is repeated as a group numerous times in succession until it is smooth, balanced, and without tension. This movement is then used in a number of the techniques we use throughout the workshop, so students not only get to practice at the beginning of class, they also get to practice during different practical applications throughout class as well.

Often on the last day and after all the students have become well practiced in this drill, we introduce a variation of the drill that is similar but unlike anything the class has done so far. Broken down to its essence, this new drill is nothing more or less than two students facing each other then performing the drill at the same time, moving toward, and then past each other as they do.

As soon as we ask the class to begin this new variation, the *dojo* suddenly fills with chatter as the students discuss with their partner how they are going to do the drill, who is going to go first, what direction they will be moving, etc. Some students stop and look around the room, watching others doing the drill. Sometimes partners run into each other. There is a lot of starting and stopping, nervous laughter, and mild chaos.

After a few minutes, we ask the students to stop. We are going to begin again, but this time, no talking. The students are also instructed to ignore everything and everybody else in the room, including their partners, and *only* focus on their own movement. We remind the students that everybody in the room has performed variations of this movement hundreds of times by now and their body knows what to do. All they need to do is let it do its job. Then I repeat, "Only focus on your movement. Don't worry about anybody or anything else."

We ask the students to begin when they're ready and each group does, almost always in slightly different intervals. But here's the interesting part. Within less than about thirty seconds, and with everyone only focusing on their own movement, *all* movement in the entire room syncs up. Without speaking, planning, counting, urging, or arranging of any kind, everybody in the room is moving as one.

We have performed this exercise all over the world, often filming the before and after results to show students the kind of positive power we can generate when we are clear about our own movement and intentions.

This is the same kind of positive power we can develop between us and our horses. By internally focusing on what we'd like from our horses instead of what they are doing (if what they are doing is not what we want) we can not only draw our horses to us, but this focus can most certainly help in the development of things such as softness, willingness, and even effortlessness of movement.

Focusing on everything *except* what we'd like from our horse, or only focusing specifically on those things we *don't* want, can have the complete opposite effect: a horse that is confused, disinterested, worried, and unresponsive.

It seemed the reason Wayne kept getting unwanted responses from his horse was because he was exclusively focusing on the arguably ill-conceived notion of trying to control his horse's thought instead of focusing on controlling his own. This was something Wayne adjusted relatively quickly and to which Marty responded in a positive way within a matter of about fifteen minutes.

The last piece to this particular puzzle has to do with something we don't really have a lot of control over. I'm referring specifically to how horses see the world and what they instinctively do so they can feel comfortable in it.

Horses possess what is referred to as a *false positive bias* when it comes to their environment. Put simply, they are designed to see everything as a potential threat until it is proven otherwise. I've heard people say that horses see humans as predators because we walk upright and have eyes in the front of our heads. Maybe. But horses also see mailboxes as predators, and rocks and shadows and streams and bridges and misplaced buckets and bicycles and rabbits and any number of other objects that don't look, sound, or smell right given the situation.

The degree to which horses are concerned with any of the above is in direct correlation to the level of life experience they have. The more horses have seen and experienced during their life, the less things in their environment are likely to bother them. The less experience they have, the more things are likely to bother them.

Wayne's horse Marty was looking around that day because he was a horse, and that's what horses do. I expect he was just familiarizing himself with his surroundings and doing so in a relatively calm way, which tells us he probably had quite a bit of positive past life experience. That's why I wasn't worried about him looking around in the first place. In fact, I would have been more concerned had he not wanted to look around a little in that new environment.

Along those same lines, I think it's important for us to understand we may be able to physically stop horses from looking around, but we won't be able to control what they think. If they aren't allowed to look, they won't be able to decide if they are safe. If they don't feel safe, they will be forced to fall back on their false positive bias. And if we think we had a problem when they were just trying to look around, we definitely aren't going to like what most likely will happen when we stop them from looking altogether.

———

Wayne was a very kind and thoughtful person who truly had his horse's best interest in mind. He was also a talented rider and good student. During that first ride, and by making a few simple adjustments concerning where he was putting his focus, he and Marty eliminated all the issues they were having with their transitions. The next day they were doing lateral movements without using any leg and by the third day they were on to flying lead changes, something that eluded the pair since Wayne bought the gelding.

As Wayne would explain during our sessions together, the concept of having a horse's *thought* was relatively new to him. He'd moved to a new barn shortly after getting Marty and had fallen in with a group of riders who all believed keeping the horse's thought on the rider was the key to good horsemanship. To hear him tell it, these riders seemed to know when a horse was worried even when the horse didn't look or act worried.

Apparently, members of the group would go out of their way to point out how worried they thought Marty looked whenever Wayne rode him. They would insist at least some of the worry was coming from Wayne not being able to get Marty's thought on him. It was for this reason that Wayne was so focused on Marty's thought when we first started that first day.

The frustration we saw from Wayne early on was coming from his inability to see or feel the things in a horse that everybody else in the group apparently could see and feel. Not wanting to look "stupid" (his word, not mine) he eventually just started to go along with whatever they said. He came to our clinic to get help improving the skills he felt he was so sorely lacking, and to do so without other members of the group telling him he was doing it wrong. By the time he decided to come to the clinic, again, to hear Wayne tell it, the folks in the group started to call into question Wayne's horsemanship skills because he "just wasn't getting it."

It's unfortunate, but a lot of what goes on in the horsemanship world these days is based on looking for the "bad" that the horse or rider might be struggling with so it can be "fixed," rather than looking for the good so it can be built on. One of the problems with this way of thinking, and there are a lot of them, is when we start looking exclusively for the "bad," it isn't long before that's all we can see—even when there is no bad to be seen—as was the case with Wayne and Marty.

Another thing I find unfortunate is the level of fault and blame that is often associated with this way of thinking. In Mary's case, she'd been convinced if her horse turned his head away when she went to halter him, she'd ruined their relationship. With Wayne, he'd been convinced his horsemanship skills were lacking because he couldn't see or feel worry in his horse that most likely wasn't even there to begin with.

It doesn't have to be that hard. And we certainly don't have to be that hard on our-selves. It's not productive.

Seems to me if we want to be successful with horses, we could start by remember-ing two simple things. The first is to just do the best we can all the time, even though our best might not be good enough all the time. The second is remembering that *horse behavior is just horse behavior.*

CHAPTER 8

The Horse's Brain

"A wise man proportions his beliefs to the evidence."

DAVID HUME

In all the time I spent with Walter, and as I mentioned previously, I never once heard him use words like "That horse needs to *respect* your space," or "She doesn't *respect* that fence," or "He has no *respect* for humans," or "You need to get that horse's *respect*," or any number of others so commonplace these days. I believe the reason he didn't use the word "respect" in relation to horses is, as I also mentioned, he understood that horse behavior is just horse behavior, and because of that, unwanted behavior was never personal nor was it intentionally adversarial. The idea of respect never entered into it.

Because I hadn't been introduced to the notion of respect in relation to horses back then, it wasn't something that even entered my consciousness as I grew and began working with horses on my own. It wasn't until I began doing clinics that I was first introduced to the idea, and even then, I didn't quite understand it.

My clinic career, such as it was, began while I was still working at the first dude ranch I managed. While at that ranch, I learned of a fledgling horse rescue in Colorado looking for training help with some of the horses they were taking in. One thing led to another and soon I accepted a couple horses from them to work with. After we'd gotten those horses in a good place, we sent them back and the rescue sent us a couple more, and so on.

As I understand it, word trickled out that I was the guy helping them with their horses, and soon I was getting calls from people the rescue referred who needed help with their horses. After about a year of this, I received a call from a woman south of Denver who owned two horses she needed help with. She said she was willing to pay for my gas to get there, pay me for my travel time, provide lunch, and pay for the work I would do with her horses. All told, she was offering almost more money for one day than I made in a month. So, I went.

When I got to her place there were the two horses I was to work with, the owner and three of her friends who wanted to watch. The issues she was having with her horses were relatively minor and we were able to get things resolved with both of them within a couple hours. The people there watching mentioned they had some horses they could use some help with, so I was invited back the next week.

When I returned, there were three or four horses and six or seven people watching. The week after that there were six or seven horses and fourteen or fifteen people. The week after that there nine horses and twenty-five people. By that time, enough people were showing up that it became difficult for them to hear what I was saying. So, at their request, I started to bring along a small PA system.

I thought I'd just been going there to work with horses, so you can imagine my surprise when one of the ladies watching told me she really liked the horsemanship clinics I'd been giving. I didn't even know there was such a thing as horsemanship clinics, much less that I was putting one on. As it turned out, that wasn't the only surprise I was in for that day.

I noticed Pam and her horse long before they came to the round pen where I was working with students. They arrived about mid-morning. Pam parked her trailer near the others and unloaded a little bay Paint mare who didn't seem too happy to be there. She was jumping around like a dancing goat on a nuclear-powered hot plate before she was even out of the trailer, and things didn't get much better from there. Tied to the trailer, the mare screamed so loud they heard her in South Dakota and pawed a hole so deep her front legs disappeared to the knees. Pam untied the mare and held her while a friend backfilled the hole, which the mare promptly re-excavated once tied back up.

When it was Pam's turn with me, she brought the Paint, Dream, into the pen. By this time, Dream was so sweaty the dirt she'd pawed all over herself turned to mud that made her look like she'd been dipped in half-melted chocolate. She was still calling and jumping around quite a bit, but what really caught my eye was what Pam carried in her hand. The thing looked like a buggy whip with what appeared to be a red handkerchief attached to one end. Today most folks in the horse world would recognize this as a "flag," but back then it was new to me.

As active as Dream was on the end of Pam's halter rope, Pam was equally active with that handkerchief-tipped stick. She flicked it this way and that with the nimbleness of an Olympian fencer, using it to whack Dream on the shoulder, neck, chest, and hip anytime she got too close.

"This is the most disrespectful horse I've ever owned," Pam said, matter-of-fact, the handkerchief on the end of the stick making a "fwapping" sound as it struck Dream's sweaty shoulder.

"I'm sorry," I said, not sure I'd heard her right. "She's what?"

"Disrespectful." Pam gave me a look as if to say *are you blind,* while at the same time "fwapping" Dream on both the chest and shoulder in quick succession. Her accuracy was impressive seeing as how she wasn't even looking at the horse at the time.

She's got some skill with that thing, I thought to myself before bringing my attention back to the question at hand.

"What does that mean, 'disrespectful'?" I asked.

What I received in answer to my question could only be described as about a ten-minute tutorial on the concept of horse respect and disrespect, not just from Pam, but from several people who were there watching as well. Explanations were lobbed in from every direction, and I listened as closely as I could to everything being said.

I was fascinated by how clear and concise the information was. It was almost like everybody was reading out of the same book at the same time. I even nodded several times to let them know I was taking in the material being presented, and I understood what they were saying.

When they finished, I nodded one last time. I didn't believe a word of what was said, but I wanted to at least do something to acknowledge the effort and energy that had just been expended in an attempt to help educate me. We then moved on to working with the mare and bypassed any more discussion on the subject.

If you would have asked me at the time why I didn't believe what they were saying, I'm not sure I'd have had an answer. It was just one of those situations when regardless of how articulate or convincing someone might sound, you just know what they're saying isn't true. Even more than knowing it, you can feel it. And I felt it.

Around this same time, the little fledgling horse-rescue operation I mentioned suddenly became very popular. It went from two women and some nine or ten rescue horses in a little six-stall barn, to forty horses, a large board of directors, the lease on a fifty-acre horse facility with hay fields, two barns, offices, and a house, as well as scores of volunteers.

The board of directors offered me the position of ranch foreman and head trainer at this new facility, which paid more than my dude ranch job and promised fewer hours, so I accepted. Unfortunately, within just a couple months of being hired, the politics within the organization made it nearly impossible for me to do the job I was hired to do, or almost any job on the place for that matter, and I chose to move on.

That was when I started my little horse training school with the Mustangs, and a few months later, began working on *Considering the Horse*. During the writing of the book was the next time I found myself discussing "respect" in relation to horses.

In one of the chapters, I talk about a few horses that struggled with ground issues. In the introduction to one of the horses, I wrote, *One of the best ways to help a horse with ground issues is to help them understand how to give to pressure.*

Scott, my editor during that project, added two sentences: *The horse has less of a training problem and more of an attitude problem.* And, *"Specifically the horse has a lack of respect for people."*

This was during the hectic time I told you about in chapter 1, when it seemed the marketing director was trying to scuttle the publication of the book, Scott was stalling the publisher to prevent another author from getting my publication slot, and I was writing as quickly as I could.

All through the process when Scott and I worked together, I was okay with most of the edits he made to the manuscript, especially during those times when I wasn't exactly sure how to communicate what I was trying to say in the first place. But I did disagree with him on this.

For a couple weeks, if I remember right, he and I went round and round about these two sentences. I didn't want them at all, and he wanted them left in because he felt they would resonate with most readers, especially those with similar problems with their horses.

I had a few things working against me during these discussions. The first was the time crunch we were under to get the book finished. The second was I couldn't come up with anything Scott felt was better, and the third was I couldn't articulate why I was so averse to using the word "respect." The sentences made it into the book.

The next time I found myself in a discussion about respect happened years later. I was still working at the second dude ranch, but by now I had two books out, *Considering the Horse* and *A Good Horse Is Never a Bad Color*. I had been contacted by a gentleman out in California who invited me to the Los Angeles area to put on a clinic.

At that clinic I found myself working with a horse that was pushy with his owner. Whenever his owner wasn't paying attention, the gelding would sidle up to her and nudge her with his head. Sometimes it would be a light bump, other times she would nearly get knocked off her feet. During our discussion about what was going on, the owner made a point to say the horse didn't do the behavior when she first got him, but that she had been hand-feeding him treats and that she liked it when he came up to her. She just didn't like him pushing.

One of the auditors, an older fella in a large straw cowboy hat, bushy eyebrows, and Sam Elliott moustache, asked why people allow their horses to become so disrespectful.

I paused before answering, trying to put my thoughts about the subject, which were minimal at the time, into coherent order. In that pause and seemingly out of nowhere, I received a sudden "download" of information that helped clear things up in my mind. This sort of thing has occurred many times throughout my years with horses and often shows up when I'm presented with an issue that has troubled me for a while and for which I haven't had an answer. Interestingly, I have spoken with other trainers, clinicians, and even authors who say they have the same or similar things happen with them. One second an issue seems insurmountable, the next everything is so clear it's like the answer has been there all along. These "downloads" of information can occur in real time and even in mid-sentence or conversation. I've even had times when I start answering a question for someone for which I don't really have an answer, when out of nowhere, well-informed information about the subject tumbles out of my mouth as if someone else is saying it. It is interesting to note that after this sort of thing happens, the new information I just imparted will stick with me, but I'll often have little or no recollection of what I said.

So, while coherent thoughts or answers about respect had escaped me in the past, this time they didn't. I began my answer with a question.

"What would you say this horse is doing that is disrespectful?" I asked.

A look of consternation crossed his face. He raised his hand in the direction of the gelding as he nudged his owner yet again. "Isn't it plain? He's all over her."

"Okay," I nodded. "And what *would* be respectful?"

"*Not* doing that." The obviousness of his statement brought a subdued chuckle from the crowd.

"So, if we teach him a boundary, say an arm's length, and he stays outside that boundary, then that would be respectful?"

"Yeah."

"You're saying respect is the horse repeating what we teach?"

"Yes."

"What if we teach him to come into our space, like this horse is doing? Respect or disrespect?"

"A horse invading someone's space is disrespectful."

"Even if we teach him to do it?"

"I don't follow."

"Horses will repeat any behavior that benefits them." I shrugged. "That's what training is, getting the horse to find and repeat a behavior for benefit. If a horse benefits from standing an arm's length from us, he'll stand an arm's length from us. If he benefits from being right on top of us, he'll do that. Right now, he's benefitting from being close to his owner. It's what she taught him. She probably didn't mean to, but he doesn't know that."

"What's the benefit for a horse standing at an arm's length?" he asked.

"Release of pressure, at least initially," I replied. "Same benefit he gets for standing too close."

I paused because it looked like he wanted to say something. He didn't, so I continued.

"I don't believe this horse is doing anything respectful or disrespectful," I said. "I see this as a misunderstanding. So, if we want him to have better boundaries, we just teach him better boundaries. Clear up the misunderstanding."

The man nodded.

This was the first of what would ultimately be countless times I would use this same or similar explanation regarding the idea of respect in relation to horses. I felt good about the explanation because it connected my belief that horse behavior is just horse behavior with the reality of cause and effect. In other words, when we teach horses a certain behavior, whether intentionally or unintentionally (cause), they will repeat that behavior (effect). The idea of respect or disrespect never enters into it.

There was one problem, though. My entire point of view was based on an opinion I fostered rather than anything I knew to be fact. So soon after the exchange in California, I decided I wanted to find actualities about how horses perceive the world around them, what makes them so amenable to training in the first place, and whether they are capable of understanding the concept of respect. The search moved along in fits and starts, ultimately becoming more involved and time-consuming than I anticipated, and probably not very interesting for anybody to want to read about here. So, suffice it to say everything I found pointed to the horse's brain and how it differs from the human brain.

I want to reiterate here that part of my focus was to find out if horses were even capable of understanding the concept of respect, and the answer I found was no, they aren't. The reason for this is simple. At the time I first began my research, it was believed that horses didn't possess a neocortex. They do. New information resulting from today's sophisticated neuroimaging seems to show the horse does have some neocortex and some prefrontal cortex. But according to neuroscientist and horse brain researcher Dr. Stephen Peters, co-author of the book *Evidence Based Horsemanship* with horseman Martin Black, these are nowhere as large, complex, or as evolved as humans and it took an extremely powerful MRI never used on horses before just to find them.

For context, the neocortex is the part of the brain that, in humans, is involved in higher functions such as language, spatial reasoning, abstract thinking, sensory perception, organization, extrapolation, categorization, conscious thought, and more. It is the part of the brain that allows us to conjure up ideas such as right and wrong, good and bad, respect and disrespect, and countless other notions a horse has no chance of understanding. So not only is it impossible for a horse to "respect" or "disrespect" us in the ways other humans might do so, demanding he does usually only sets up an adversarial situation that puts him on the defensive and causes him to want to get as far away from us as he can. The recent discovery that horses seem to possess some semblance of a neocortex and prefrontal cortex does not change this fact.

In my book *Finding the Missed Path: The Art of Restarting Horses* I dedicated an entire chapter to debunking the idea that horses can understand respect and disrespect. Sometime after the book's release, I received an email from Dr. Peters saying he wanted to let me know he read my book and that from a scientific standpoint, the chapter on debunking respect was "right on the money."

That email ultimately led to Crissi and I, as well as our senior student instructor Gray Graves and a few others to attend an informal talk on the horse's brain that Dr. Peters was giving at his house. For three hours, we were immersed in an amazing power-point presentation covering all aspects of equine neuroscience and chemistry. After the presentation, Crissi, Gray, and I ended up staying another two hours talking with Dr. Peters about horse behavior and how it all ties back to brain function.

We just happened to be doing a clinic nearby with the last day of the clinic starting at nine the next morning. As a direct result of the night going a little longer than anticipated, the morning seemed to arrive much faster than expected. Because of that, I was almost, but not quite, fully awake when I went out around half past seven to feed our horses.

Their pen wasn't far from where our living quarters trailer was parked, maybe fifty feet or so. As I stepped out of the trailer that morning, I threw a casual glance toward the pen. I do this more out of habit than anything else to make sure everybody is still upright and no obvious injuries occurred overnight. This glance seldom lasts more than a second or two, just long enough to make sure nothing out of the ordinary registers, before I'm off to load hay into the portable cart we travel with and that I then wheel to the horses.

A bit groggy and with information from the night before still careening around in my head, I tossed a few flakes of hay over the fence near the horses, then moved down the fence and tossed the rest. I scooped up the remaining remnants of hay from the bottom of the cart and tossed that as well. It was about then that something unexpected happened.

I looked up at the horses. This wasn't the casual glance from earlier, but a more deliberate, top-to-bottom scan and it struck me almost immediately that something was different. The horses were the same and there weren't any injuries or wounds, although I wouldn't expect any with these two as they are long-time traveling partners. The difference wasn't with the horses, but with me.

As I watched them, I slowly realized the information Dr. Peters offered the night before was having much more of an effect on me than I thought. At the risk of sounding overly dramatic, I felt as though I was seeing our horses with more clarity than ever before. It was as if I had been looking at the same slightly blurry black-and-white photograph for years and years, and suddenly the photo came into focus and turned to color.

It dawned on me that guessing what a horse is thinking or being able to predict a horse's behavior accurately based on repetitive observed patterns is one thing. Having some understanding of the neuroscience behind what is occurring in the horse's brain during those times is quite another.

In the early 2000s, I was part of a conference in which a number of professionals in the horse industry were presenting. These included chiropractors, farriers, vets, dentists, bodyworkers, and two trainers—myself and a friend. We all gave presentations over the three days, and on the last day, we participated in a round-table discussion for the attendees.

At some point a question was asked of my friend and me having to do with developing patience when working with horses. My friend admitted that his patience only went so far, saying he would rather get on a student's horse and work out an issue with the horse himself rather than watch the student and the horse struggle together. He then went on to say that he is sometimes more apt to get in and just get a change from a troubled horse rather than wait for the horse to work out a solution.

"Mark's got more patience than me," he said half joking, half serious. "It can be hard for me to watch him sometimes. It's like watching grass grow."

This got a laugh from the crowd. As the chuckling subsided, a man in the middle of the group raised his hand. My friend called on him.

"I wouldn't say watching him work with horses is like watching grass grow. I'd say it's like watching cement set."

Another, much louder laugh burst from the crowd.

"Hold on, hold on," the man said, standing up. Laughter quieted. "I'm a building contractor, and the most important part of any building is the foundation. If the cement you use isn't the right consistency, or it isn't poured correctly, or it isn't allowed to set properly, the foundation eventually fails and whatever you've built on it fails, too." He paused. "So, watching Mark is like watching cement set. It's getting the foundation right."

As he sat down, all eyes went from him to my friend.

"Good analogy," my friend said, then paused. "But it's like watching grass grow, too."

My friend wasn't wrong. It's no secret that I'm more apt to take my time with a horse than hurry through things. Which isn't to say that I haven't had times when I've gone too fast with a horse, because Lord knows I've done that too. But in general,

I've always just found that the slower I went, the more I saw, and the more I saw, the more I learned.

This all began back at Walter's place when there were never any time constraints on anything he did. I'd watch him work with a troubled horse until he got some change, often so small that most of the time only *he* saw it. Then he'd light a cigarette, step back and watch, giving the horse time to process. Usually, the horse would eventually drop their head and yawn, or lick and chew, or rub their nose on their leg, or shake their head or offer any number of other behaviors I'm sure he inherently knew meant the horse was trying to feel better.

This kind of slower approach eventually went with me as I began to develop my own way of being with horses. Over time, and like everybody else who spends a lot of time with them, I started picking up on the little things horses do just before they are getting ready to do something else. Those little things would eventually begin to dictate my response, which more times than not might be to step back and watch. Other times it might mean that I step in and direct, and still other times it might mean that I do something in between.

I guess the point here is just through the sheer number of repetitive observed behaviors, many of us have learned to distinguish between when horses are calm and relaxed, when they are becoming worried, when they are overly stressed, when they are moving toward panic, or when they are *in* a panic. By the same token, we also learn when horses are panicked but trying to calm down, overly stressed but trying to move toward worried, or moving from worried to calm and relaxed.

I feel these are tremendously important skills for any horseperson to develop. When honed, polished, and used properly, they can go a long way to us helping keep a horse out of emotional trouble, or helping the horse get out of trouble once there. Many are the horsemen and women who are so good at these skills that they appear to know what the horse is going to do even before the horse knows. And that's a good thing.

Speaking strictly for myself (and knowing what I know now) I feel the downside to possessing this skill set without knowing at least some of the neuroscience behind it is a bit like a great musician who doesn't understand music theory or read music. Don't get me wrong, playing by ear has its benefits, for sure—the ability to improvise being at the top of the list. But understanding the hows and whys behind what people are playing not only allows them to connect all the various pieces into coherent order, but also allows the players to be much more versatile as well.

It's been the same for me when it comes to understanding something about the horse's brain function. Doing so has helped me connect the various pieces of possible causes of horse behavior and has also helped me become more versatile in my approach. The good news is one doesn't have to be an equine neuroscientist to pick up a basic knowledge as to what makes horses tick, thus gaining a deeper understanding of them.

As already mentioned, horses don't possess much of a neocortex, the big frontal lobe that makes humans, human. This is important because horses are incapable of thinking and understanding the world and their surroundings the same way we do. Projecting human beliefs and traits on them only serves to put us and them at a disadvantage when it comes to developing any meaningful communication.

Another piece of the puzzle is understanding the two divisions of the horse's *autonomic nervous* system. These are the *sympathetic* and *parasympathetic* systems. The parasympathetic is related in part to relaxation in the horse, while the sympathetic is related in part to fear responses. Having a basic knowledge of these two systems can make a big difference in the level of success we achieve when working with our horses.

As an example of how the autonomic nervous system works, let's put it on a scale from "0" to "10." We'll say "0" to "6.5" on that scale represents the parasympathetic system, "7" to "10" represents the sympathetic. For our purposes, "0" would be the horse sleeping, "10" would be the horse in a full-blown panic. The closer to "0" the horse is on this scale, the less stress the horse feels; the closer to "7" the horse gets, the more stress the horse feels.

Horses, like people, need to be under a manageable level of stress to learn. Little or no stress won't cause them to want to seek an answer to their situation. Too much stress or worry will cause them to want to flee (or fight), in which case learning is out of the question anyway. To that end, and using our scale, the optimal range for learning would be, say, in the "3.5" to "5.5" range. It's highly unlikely any learning will take place at a "2" or less or at a "7.5" or more.

Here's a situation most of us can probably relate to. Let's say we're riding in an arena the horse is used to. Parked outside the fence on one end of the arena is a tractor that has never been parked there before. Everything is fine as we begin our ride. On our scale, the horse is at a "3," attentive but not worried. As we continue our ride, and not thinking anything about the tractor because we know our horse has seen it before (although not in this context) we start for the other end of the arena.

About halfway from where we started and where the tractor sits, our horse suddenly becomes very aware. The horse goes from a "3" to a "5.5." At this point our horse is now in a slightly elevated state, but the ability to learn is still available. We now have options available to us to keep the horse in that learning frame of mind...or not. We could turn them around, go back to where we started and then come back to about the same place and see how they feel. Maybe they go down to a "5" or a "4.5," which tells us the horse is trying to feel better. Maybe they stay at a "5.5" or even go to a "6," which tells us the horse is still bothered by what they are seeing. Either way, we are taking in information while at the same time keeping them from going to a "7" (sympathetic system) or higher.

In a case like this, by simply making the effort to keep the horse under a "6.5" and allowing them time to get used to this new and unfamiliar thing, chances are they'll eventually build up enough curiosity to where they might even want to take us right over to the tractor. The horse was asking us an important question the entire time: *Am I safe?* By our actions, we answered, *Yes, you are.*

Now I'm sure there's someone out there thinking, *but my horse has been in that arena a thousand times, and has seen that tractor just as much.* Yes. But never the two together. Remember, horses don't have a neocortex like ours, it is much smaller and less complex, so they don't have the ability to extrapolate. In other words, it's near impossible for our horse, especially one with limited life experience, to work out the equation "arena + tractor = arena and tractor." In the horse's world, the arena *always* looks like the arena. Anything that shows up that's never been there before will most likely cause that false positive bias to kick in. Until proven otherwise, the new thing is a threat.

Which brings us to the second, often more common option of what to do in this situation. Put simply, we ignore the horse's concern and just ride up to the tractor to show it's nothing to worry about. In this case, the closer we get to the tractor, the higher the horse's anxiety. They go from a "5.5" to a "6," then "6.5," then "7." Once at "7" we start to get unwanted behavior. The horse stops, tries to turn around… maybe tries to back away.

It's just a tractor, we tell the horse in a calm, or maybe not-so-calm voice. They're not interested. They're asking, *Am I safe?* By our actions, we are telling them, *No, you are most definitely not safe.*

We kick their sides, urging them forward. The horse skips the "7.5" and goes straight to an "8." They try to spin, but we're able to stop them. Besides, we're only about twenty feet away now. They'll figure it out. A couple more spins and now we're ten feet from the tractor. The horse skips going to an "8.5" or even a "9" and goes straight to a "10." All bets are off.

We're on the ground without any idea of how we got there and through dirt-filled eyes, we're watching our horse run for the other end of the arena. Once there, the horse runs the fence line, head and tail high, sweat dripping from their belly and calling loudly. The horses at the barn frantically call back.

Bad horse.

For years, I have stressed the importance of helping the inside of the horse feel good enough about what is being asked so the outside of the horse will willingly go along. Looking back, I was using the term "inside of the horse" in a sort of a global sense. Meaning, I saw it as encompassing outward responses in the body as potential signs of how the inside might be feeling.

I would watch for things like normal respiration, lack of anxiety and muscle tension, and the like. Admittedly, I gave very little thought to what may have been going on in the horse's brain, primarily because my knowledge of brain function was limited and because the things we were doing seemed to be working.

As has been the case throughout my time with horses, if what I was doing was working and not troubling the horse too much, I saw no reason to overthink it. But again, this way of going probably falls into the category of the musician who doesn't understand music theory—we can get along to a point, but ultimately, options become limited.

After spending time with Dr. Peters, I came to understand that what I was unknowingly doing by "helping the inside of the horse feel good" was setting the horse's brain up to successfully receive and process information. This process begins with making sure the horse is in a productive state of mind for learning. For this, all we need to do is go back to our scale of "0" to "10," remembering we're looking for the horse to be roughly in the "3.5" to "5.5" range. We might refer to this as *relaxed alertness* or *interested but not worried.*

Then, we want to pick a task to teach our horse. It could be any task because the process is the same across the board, but for our purposes here, let's use backing up while on the horse's back. So, we softly pick up the reins and apply the amount of pressure we'd like the horse to ultimately respond to. Using another scale from "0" to "10" with "0" being no pressure and "10" being way more than we would ever want to use, we apply pressure at, say, "1," while making sure we are not pulling. By not pulling, the pressure we're offering is just a presence rather than something scary to be defended against.

To feel what pressure without pulling might feel like to the horse, all we need to do is tie a rope to a post and then pull on the rope. The harder we pull, the more pressure we will feel. In this case, the post isn't causing the increase in pressure, we are because we are moving away from the post, which isn't moving at all. When we apply pressure without pulling, we are in a sense acting like the post. Of course, we have more life than a post, but the concept is the same. Because the post isn't moving, the release is already built in and all we need to do to find that release is move toward the post.

Just like the post, if we apply pressure to the reins without pulling, the release is already built in. All the horse needs to do is go toward our hands (give to pressure) to find the release. However, a horse that doesn't initially understand how to look for a release may lean into the pressure, causing the pressure to increase.

This increase in pressure, or perhaps just feeling the pressure in the first place, usually triggers the horse's *seek system.* This is the system horses need to use to find a solution to the problem. After a time, and through trial and error, horses find the release and when they do, they get a shot of *dopamine*, a neurotransmitter associated with reward. The dopamine makes horses feel good so the next time they feel the same or similar pressure, they will look to replicate the behavior that got them the release and the dopamine hit.

One of the keys here is to give horses a little time before repeating the request. This should be enough time for them to mull over what just happened (long enough to get a lick and chew, lower or shake their head, yawn) but not so long they become disinterested or distracted.

Most of us have been taught the *release* is what teaches, but that's only partially true. The release begins the learning process, but it's the *relief* the horse gets after finding the release that allows the actual learning to take place. The release initially triggers the dopamine hit, relief allows for *dendrite* growth—the formation of new neuropathways—and it is the dendrite growth that allows for the assimilation of information.

Chances are most folks who've worked with horses for a long time have stumbled on the fact that giving breaks when horses are learning something new allows them to learn faster. Certainly, faster than mindless nonstop repetition, which has no real value to horses once they've figured out what we're asking. It's why Walter would step back and light a cigarette when working with his horses. It's why I ask riders to stop and sit for a few minutes after their horses have offered something close to what they're looking for. It's why horses that struggled with new information one day seem to magically understand it the next.

I didn't know about the process occurring in the brain when I would give a horse a break, and I'm sure Walter didn't either. What I did know is doing so almost always helped the training go much smoother. By the same token, I'd also found out the hard way when I didn't give breaks, or when I pushed harder than I should have (unknowingly driving the horse into their sympathetic nervous system), things seldom went well.

I think most of us know horses don't learn well when they're in a constant state of stress. What we may not know is keeping horses in their sympathetic system, whether intentionally or unintentionally, can actually "trim back" dendrites in the brain. In other words, we can reverse positive gains when we don't help or allow a horse to downregulate to their parasympathetic nervous system during training.

This ties back into what can happen when people believe horses are being disrespectful. For a lot of people, a disrespectful horse is a bad horse, and a bad horse needs to be disciplined. Here's the problem. By the time a horse is deemed disrespectful, they are probably already in or approaching being in their sympathetic nervous system. Upping the pressure will only serve to make sure they get in and stay in their sympathetic system.

Another problem here is disciplining usually equates to punishment driven by emotion, specifically fear, frustration, or anger. These emotions in the human are almost always connected to a loss of self-control, which is connected to a loss of awareness. Loss of awareness creates a loss of feel and timing. When this happens, even if the horse is trying to search for a release from the punishment, the person delivering it can't see or feel their try.

This can lead to another issue. *Learned helplessness.* If a horse is presented with a situation for which they are unable to find a release or a solution, more times than not they will emotionally shut down. This can appear as though the horse is being cooperative when really what we've done is short circuit their ability to learn by pushing them into a state of disassociation.

These horses can look just fine and even act like everything is okay, but they're not. At some point, usually at the most inopportune time, they snap out of it. When they do, seldom if ever will they go right into their parasympathetic nervous system. More likely they'll go back into their sympathetic system first.

Look at it as if we've added a number to our nervous system scale of "0" to "10." This new number, "11," is beyond panic and is the result of the horse being pushed into learned helplessness. For the horse to get back into their parasympathetic system, they can't just go from "11" to "6.5." Rather, they must go from "11" to "10." This means the first thing a shutdown horse will usually do when they "wake up" is panic.

A very similar thing happens to people who go under anesthesia while they're panicking. The person goes under just fine, but when the person wakes up, they do so in the same state in which they went under. It's like their panic had simply been suspended, only to resume in full force once conscious again.

Here's the good news. We can avoid all of this with our horses, and all it takes is a little knowledge, skill, and mindfulness. Learning how to keep our horses in their parasympathetic system when showing them new things or skills is the key. Knowing how to help horses downregulate out of the sympathetic once they are there is also a handy skill. Luckily, one of the easiest ways to do that is to simply give them (and us) a break before things get too far out of hand.

A few years back Dr. Peters, Jim Masterson, founder of the Masterson Method equine body work, and I were doing a joint seminar around the research Dr. Peters had gathered regarding horse brain function. The idea was for Dr. Peters to give his power-point presentation about brain science and chemistry, then Jim and I would offer demonstrations with horses, and Dr. Peters would add commentary about what was taking place in the horse's brain. I would be using two different horses during my demonstration time. One was a troubled mare I did some groundwork with; the other was a riding demonstration with my solid clinic horse, Rocky.

I was supposed to do both demonstrations in an outdoor round pen but was only able to get the groundwork demonstration in as a storm suddenly rolled in from the west while I was finishing up with the mare. We quickly moved everything and everybody into the nearby indoor arena as the wind picked up and rain began pouring down.

At the time of this seminar, Rocky and I had been together for fifteen years. During that time, we had traveled about a million miles and been in countless situations where we'd learned to depend on one another. It was difficult to find a situation in which Rocky wasn't comfortable, but as it turned out, this was one of them.

I brought Rocky into the arena and mounted up just as the worst of the storm hit. Strong gusts of wind rattled the walls, doors, and roof of the building while rain pounded down so hard that it was difficult to hear even with the PA system we were using.

Almost immediately, Rocky's anxiety began to climb, but as I spoke to the attendees, I did what I always did when he got worried. I gave him some direction. In this case we did a series of large and small circles, serpentines, and figure eights. Pretty soon he calmed down and we went on with the demonstration, which was on combining the horse's sensitivity and our energy to develop invisible aids.

Rocky and I would stop from time to time to answer questions while the wind and rain continued outside. It was during one of these pauses that Dr. Peters, who was also wearing a mic, interjected. He asked the attendees to take note of what Rocky was doing while I answered their questions.

I'm going to stop for a second here and add a couple things about Rocky and my relationship. He came to us when he was seven from a little cattle ranch in Minnesota.

His life experiences up to that point had been positive but relatively limited. When we started traveling together, I found there were a lot of things he would become troubled by because he had no experience with them. In these situations, my primary concern was always finding something I could do to help him feel better.

To that end, and depending on the situation, I might do what I did on this day—give him direction until I felt his worried energy subside. Other times, I might get him away from the thing that was worrying him. Still other times, I might just get off him, especially if I felt I might somehow be the cause of his worry.

The longer we were together, the more confidence we developed in each other and the less I found I needed to help him. By the time of this demonstration, there wasn't too much that bothered him anymore. When something did bother him, as it did on this day, I would just fall back on giving him a little direction and soon enough, he'd usually feel better.

But Dr. Peters had picked up on something else. Anytime a loud or unexpected noise would happen, Rocky would tighten, his head would come up, sometimes he would call out. All of this was quickly followed by him lowering his head, yawning, licking, and chewing, or rubbing his nose on his front legs.

"Rocky doesn't need Mark anymore," Dr. Peters said. "Watch what he's doing. Whenever he starts to get worried, he downregulates on his own. He's keeping himself from going to his sympathetic nervous system."

He went on to say that I had helped Rocky downregulate enough times throughout our time together that he now knew how to get there on his own. He was able to influence his own brain chemistry in a positive way.

"Whenever Rocky asked the question, *Am I safe?*" Dr. Peters added. "The answer he always got was, *Yes, you're safe.*"

Nobody knows what a horse is really thinking. But now that Rocky is gone, I'd kind of like to believe he really did feel safe with me. I know I felt safe with him.

CHAPTER 9

New Revelations

*"An open mind leaves a chance for someone
to drop a worthwhile thought in it."*

MARK TWAIN

There was a time early on when I believed all troubled horses could be rehabilitated. I'm sure this idea came from my time with Walter. Almost all the horses he took in back then were troubled, and he was always able to get them to a better place. As I branched out on my own, however, I started running into the occasional horse that caused me to question that notion.

Back in the mid-1980s I received a call from Elaine, an experienced horsewoman I'd done a little work for in the past who said she needed help with a colt she was trying to get started. Elaine raised and started most of her own youngsters but had picked up this particular colt at a sale a few months before.

"He's really well bred," she said during our phone conversation. "But I'm having trouble getting along with him. I must be missing something."

I told her I'd be happy to help if I could and a few days later was over at her place. He was in the round pen eating from a hay net when I arrived, a three-year-old sorrel gelding with three white socks and a marking on his forehead that looked like a flying ghost. His barn name was Casper.

Elaine told me she had been working with him for almost a month and had barely made any headway at all. This was a bit surprising because Elaine grew up with horses, was known for her gentle and quiet way with them, and had started hundreds of youngsters over the years, many of them going on to become big money earners on various show circuits.

"Some colts take longer than others," she said. "But this one is different."

She went on to explain she would show him something one day, such as lungeing, and he would seem to do well with it. The next day, or the day after, or sometimes even a week later, he would suddenly act as if he'd never done it before. Sometimes, he would even act like he'd never even seen the lunge rope before. Inevitably, she would have to start the whole process over, he would seem to do well, and then next time they'd be right back where they started. As a result, she hadn't gotten very far with him.

She said she had yet to see him canter. He didn't canter in the pasture, even when the other colts were running and he was trying to keep up, and she couldn't get him to canter in the round pen on those days when she was able to lunge him. She had the vet look at him, but he couldn't find anything wrong.

"He's really sweet," she added. "Except when he's not."

"What do you mean?"

"Well," she said as she leaned on the round pen fence. "The other day we finished working and everything seemed fine. I was winding up the lunge rope and he was standing over there, quiet as a church mouse." She pointed to a spot on the other side of the pen. "Out of the blue, he wheeled and came at me, ears back, teeth showing. I used the rope to get him turned, but he seemed pretty serious. After that, he just went back over there and acted like nothing happened."

We stood watching the colt eat when, as if on cue, he pinned his ears, wheeled, and charged. I clapped my hands when he got close, causing him to veer off before reaching either of us. He made a small circle, then charged again. Another hand clap was enough to turn him a second time. He trotted back to the hay net and went back to eating.

"Is that what he does?" I asked.

"Yup. And it seems to be getting worse lately."

There's an old adage that says there aren't any coincidences. Still, it just so happened a couple weeks before this, I was reading an article in some magazine while waiting in the dentist's office about the effects inbreeding was having on purebred dogs. Among other things, this article talked about how many inbred dogs ended up with learning deficits, coordination issues, and random aggressiveness—the same behaviors that seemed to be going on with this horse.

I mentioned the article to Elaine and asked her if she knew the horse's lineage. She said she glanced at his registration papers after buying him, but then sent them in to the breeders association to get transferred. The new papers hadn't been returned to her yet. After a brief discussion, Elaine decided to hold off on any more training until the colt's papers came back and she could look a little deeper into his breeding.

A few weeks later, Elaine called again to let me know his papers had come back, and on closer inspection she found that he was, indeed, inbred. The same sire crossed with his own offspring showed up twice on the colt's dam side and once on his sire's side. Having done a little more digging, she found that other horses from these lines were known to have similar handling and training issues. Some were so bad that training was completely abandoned, and those horses were often then used for breeding stock.

This was the first time I came across a horse whose behavioral issues could be tied directly back to its breeding. It wouldn't be the last.

I was first invited to do clinics in England in the late 1990s, and I have been back numerous times since. Crissi often accompanies me, and often on our days off, our hosts have been kind enough to take us sightseeing. These trips have included visiting prehistoric places such as Stonehenge and the less well known (at least to those here in the United States) Avebury henge.

Nobody really knows for sure why sites like this were built, but a popular belief is they were constructed around specific astronomical alignments that only occur at very specific times throughout the year. This is fascinating to me, especially if true, because unlike here in Colorado where clear night skies are more common than not, clear night skies in England are far less common. Assuming the same was the case in ancient times, it must have taken hundreds, if not thousands of years for the folks back then to pinpoint exactly when those astronomical alignments occurred due simply to those times when cloud cover obscured their night sky view.

According to the *Merriam-Webster Online Dictionary*, the word "empirical" means "information acquired by observation or experimentation." The time it took those folks to gather enough empirical evidence to get the alignments correct is one thing. But then to be confident enough in their data to drag huge stones excavated by hand from hundreds of miles away so that massive henges could be constructed based on those alignments is quite another.

It turns out we all make decisions based on empirical evidence every day. Maybe not huge stone-dragging, henge-building decisions, but decisions nonetheless. Whether that decision is choosing the best way to get across town, how long to bake a pie without burning it, or knowing to avoid hitting our thumb with a hammer, empirical evidence most definitely plays an important role in our lives.

This kind of evidence is especially handy when it comes to working with horses. We learn to trust through observation that certain behavior in horses usually follows certain motivators. Because of that, when training or working with them we can make informed decisions around potential responses to the kind of behavior that will likely follow that motivator.

Most specifically, though, when we see unwanted behavioral patterns that can consistently be linked with, say, inbreeding in a horse's documented lineage, we can say with some certainty the behavior has something to do with the breeding. By the same token, we can also assume, through our empirical evidence, when we see those exact same behaviors in horses where the lineage cannot be verified, the behavior may also be caused by a breeding issue.

Before going any further, I should probably point out in the forty or so years since making the connection between the behavior Elaine's colt was exhibiting and inbreeding in his lineage, we have seen hundreds of other horses in the same boat. The behaviors we've noticed most consistently in these horses have been their inability to retain information, trouble with coordination (particularly the faster they go), an

unusual amount of trouble adapting to new environments, aggressiveness, and being overly reactive in even the most mundane of situations. Some horses we've seen
possessed all these traits (and a few more) while others might only exhibit just one or
two. We've also noticed there can be a wide range of degrees in these behaviors from
one horse to the next.

As an example, we have seen horses like Elaine's colt who were completely unable
to progress past some of the most basic learning skills, while others are able to be ridden, although just barely. Still others can be worked and ridden at a very high level,
whether in the show ring, working cattle, or whatever.

To illustrate the variety of degrees of behaviors in these horses, Crissi bought a little
Missouri Foxtrotter a few years back that she called Banjo. Banjo is registered with
inbreeding in his recent lineage. However, Banjo wasn't started under saddle until he
was seven years old, and when he was started, it was done slowly and thoughtfully.
Banjo was used mostly for trail rides and working cattle, both of which he did very
well. Because the previous owner was going off to college, she decided to look for a
new home for him, which is how Crissi ended up with him.

Banjo has proven himself to be a solid ranch, trail, and clinic horse. However, he
can be a bit "quirky" as Crissi refers to it. For example, during the summer months
while teaching our ten-day intensive clinics, we need to bring our horses through a
specific area to get them tacked up. This area is between two trailers parked about
twenty feet apart. One of the trailers casts a shadow that shades the open area between
the two. Every day, without fail, whenever Crissi asks Banjo to enter that area he stops,
drops his head, and snorts as if he's never seen it before. When he finally does enter
the area, which can take some time, he does so as if he's walking on hot coals.

In another instance, Banjo had been traveling with us on the road for three years
and not once had he showed signs of being troubled about going in or coming out of
the trailer. That is, until one morning in New Mexico on our way to Arizona when
we went to load him. Out of the blue, he stopped at the back of the trailer and acted
as if he'd never seen it before. We had to help him figure everything out again, which
he did, and he hasn't had any trouble since.

On the other end of the spectrum is a horse we saw at a clinic out on the East
Coast. It was there that a woman brought a gelding in who seemed to be in a

full-blown panic, charging circles around her, screaming at the top of his lungs, and spooking at everything.

To her credit, the woman remained calm, giving him direction when she could and acting as if this was an everyday occurrence. When I asked her if what we were seeing was normal for this horse, she said it was, especially when the gelding was in a new or unfamiliar place.

"It can be worse," she said in a composed voice as the gelding whipped past her. He then stopped, rocked back on his haunches, and launched himself in the other direction, eyes wide and screaming in full voice. "But it's seldom better."

She went on to say that she could ride him, but only at home and only in places where he was comfortable. Even then there were times when, out of nowhere, he would just explode. She said he had always had trouble retaining information and didn't do well with new things, places, or people. She had vets look at him, trainers, bodyworkers, dentists, saddle fitters, a top-notch farrier, along with being very mindful about his nutrition, and nothing really seemed to help.

Someone in the crowd got out of a chair, which caused the gelding to spook and bolt toward the woman. She skillfully sidestepped him, and as he flew past, she turned her attention back to me.

"Do you happen to know how he's bred?" I asked.

"I do," she replied, matter-of-fact. "He's inbred. I have his papers. Oh, I forgot to mention, he also has a degenerative bone disease, and the vet said his skull is deteriorating."

I explained to her that, under the circumstances, I didn't believe there was anything I could do for him from a training standpoint. The issues he had were textbook as far as what I had seen in other inbred horses over the years and, to my knowledge, there wasn't any way to fix or reverse what he had going on.

Interestingly, the woman said she had pretty much already come to that same conclusion, but she just wanted to get a second opinion. She then asked for suggestions on what they might be able to do together going forward. I suggested they keep things simple, and just do what he was comfortable doing.

"Do what you can do and stay away from things you can't," was my advice. "I doubt he'll let you do anything else, anyway."

"Yeah," she agreed. "He's been pretty clear about that."

During the 1990s and through the early 2000s, we began seeing a rash of young, un-registered horses at our clinics who all seemed to exhibit the types of behaviors common in inbred horses. These youngsters were made up primarily of grade Quarter Horse types and Draft Horse crosses. The one common denominator was almost all had been what is referred to as PMU babies. For those who don't know, PMU is short for (P)regnant (M)are (U)rine, from which the female hormone Premarin® is derived. At the time, urine for the industry was being collected from pregnant mares on farms and ranches all over Canada and North Dakota. Because the primary concern of this industry was the urine and not the foal, many (not all) of the foals from these mares, once weaned, were fattened up and shipped off to slaughter. In the 1990s, a big push was implemented to rescue these slaughter-bound babies and as a result, a large number were eventually adopted out in the United States.

Unfortunately, foals from the industry back then were frequently looked on by the producer as a byproduct that was ultimately going to be disposed of anyway. As a result, not a lot of care had been given by some of the producers as to which stallions were covering which mares. According to an acquaintance who was involved in the industry at the time, this often resulted in a good deal of inbreeding.

I'd like to be very clear here that not all PMU babies were inbred. In fact, there were a number of farms and ranches involved in Premarin production that were not only using responsible breeding practices, but several were even raising, training, and selling registered Quarter Horses. I know of at least one PMU baby that did so well on the show circuit that he ultimately qualified for the American Quarter Horse Association's World Championship.

Also, it's important to keep in mind people don't usually bring horses to us when they are going well. We usually see horses and owners who are struggling a bit. As a result, our perspective of inbreeding in PMU babies is somewhat skewed because those were the majority of what we were seeing.

The common complaints owners of these youngsters had back then ranged from, again, the colt's inability to retain information, coordination issues, aggressiveness, being overreactive in new or unfamiliar situations, and just over-all unpredictability. Most of the owners mentioned the issues didn't really come to light until they tried to start the colt under saddle, or when they would ask the horse to do anything other than be led from one place to another.

I recall one of these youngsters whose training was going extremely slowly, ac-cording to the owner. Among other things, this owner said her colt could be led forward with a halter and rope but would refuse to back up when asked. When she demonstrated what was going on, she applied a little pressure to the halter rope and the young gelding responded by tucking his head and plowing forward, dragging her with him. The response looked defensive to me, and I wondered if perhaps using less pressure would help him feel less inclined to push into it.

I asked the owner if she minded if I gave it a try, to which she happily handed me the rope. I stood at the colt's right side, petted him on the neck, and then ap-plied gentle backward pressure on the halter rope. On our scale from "0" to "10" with "0" being no pressure and "10" being way more than we would ever want to use, the pressure I applied was at about a "0.5."

The good news was the colt didn't plow forward. The not-so-good news was it seemed as though he couldn't feel the pressure at all. His expression didn't change and there was no response anywhere in his body. I decided to wait a short while longer without increasing or releasing the pressure. Still no response.

After about ten seconds, I added a hair more pressure, going from "0.5" to "0.75." To be accurate when using this level of pressure, the increase had to be done very slowly, otherwise it would be easy to apply more pressure than I want-ed. Besides, there was a chance the horse might want to respond at "0.65," and if I applied the pressure too quickly, I wouldn't be able to feel if he did.

Because of this I try to be very aware of the small, smooth, incremental movement I use when increasing pressure at this level, as well as any potential response the horse might be thinking about offering. I mention all of this because I want to emphasize just how little it took to elicit the behavior that happened next.

Initially, I felt no response whatsoever from the colt as I slowly increased the pres-sure. I went from "0.5" to "0.55," to "0.60," to "0.65," and still nothing. Then, at "0.70," and with no change in expression, no tightening of the body, no change of feel in the rope, the colt suddenly struck out with his right front foot, the one closest to me. This was not what we might refer to as a typical strike where the foot and leg are thrust almost directly forward, but rather this appeared to be much more thoughtful and deliberate.

My right hand, the hand with which I was applying the pressure was about eight or ten inches from the bottom of the colt's jaw. With this strike, the colt had to draw his leg back, then lift it high enough to get his foot above and over the top of my arm and hand, then strike downward, effectively sweeping my hand free of the rope. Mind you, I never actually saw any of that. It all happened so fast—one moment my hand was on the rope, the next it wasn't. I barely even saw the horse's leg move before it was back on the ground. Luckily, I was holding the rope loosely enough that when the strike happened, my hand easily fell away. Had I been gripping the rope tightly, I probably would have gotten hurt.

I bring up this particular situation because it is just one example of the kinds of unpredictable and often explosive reactions we've seen from inbred horses, even when being asked to do the simplest of tasks. And unfortunately, this was mild compared to some of the behaviors we've seen.

Around this same time, we came across another PMU horse during a clinic, a mare, who's behavior was so abnormal the word "dangerous" doesn't come close to describing it.

This clinic was held in an indoor arena with some thirty or forty auditors present. I worked with riders on one end of the arena and on the other end was a round pen. The round pen sat empty for most of the day, but about midafternoon, a Paint mare showed up and was placed in the pen. The mare was owned by a woman we'll call Cathy.

I had known Cathy for several years, and we'd even worked together three or four times in the past. She grew up around horses, and it showed, being equally handy with saddle horses and draft horses. Most of the horses she owned had some size to them, being mostly Draft or Draft crosses, which is why I was a bit surprised to see this mare, who stood just a little over fourteen hands.

While working with the riders on one end of the arena, I would glance at the mare in the round pen from time to time. From that distance, and as she walked around the inside of the pen, I couldn't really see anything out of the ordinary. Not at first, anyway. She had nice coloring and markings, good conformation, and appeared to be moving freely with a symmetrical stride.

Still, something about her caused me to keep looking her way. My glances went from just a second or two, to five or six seconds to eventually a half-minute or more at a time. Between riders, and if I wasn't answering questions from the auditors, I would find myself staring at the mare as she walked the pen. The longer I watched, the more I got the impression something wasn't right, although I couldn't tell exactly what.

When it came Cathy's turn, I made my way down to the round pen followed by all the auditors who took up spots around the pen to watch. The mare was still moving as I walked up, and as I got close, the thing that didn't look right to me suddenly became clear. I got the distinct impression this mare wasn't just ambling around. She looked to be *prowling,* almost like a big cat on the hunt.

All the movement was there, the way she shaped her body through turns, the way she held her head, the cold in her eyes as she scanned the auditors outside the pen. I've noticed this look in all kinds of predators over the years, from our little house cat hunting in the yard, to coyotes, bears, lions, and on and on. It was a look I'd not seen in a horse, or any prey animal for that matter, which is why I was having trouble putting my finger on what I was seeing.

Almost as soon as that thought crossed my mind, I tried to push it aside. I knew nothing about this horse and the last thing I wanted to do was taint my view of her before I even knew why she was there. Besides, there was certainly the chance that my imagination was playing tricks on me.

As I listened to Cathy explain why she had brought the mare, however, I started to realize perhaps it wasn't my imagination after all. She was a six- or seven-year-old PMU out of Canada that had been passed around to different owners due to her aggressiveness. She attacked numerous people putting several in the hospital with broken bones, including the woman Cathy got her from, who suffered a broken arm when the mare grabbed and shook her by it. That owner gave her to Cathy in hopes she could be rehabilitated.

Cathy said the mare had come after her several times as well, but so far, she had been lucky enough to fend her off without being injured. She said at one point, she was in the paddock with her horses, including this mare, when the mare suddenly charged from some thirty or forty feet away.

"It happened so fast," she said. "I didn't have time to react. What saved me was one of my other horses ran at her and knocked her off her feet before she could get to me."

Cathy said she'd been working with the mare for over a year, had tried everything she knew to help the mare feel better, including positive reinforcement, being kind, being firm, changing feed, bodywork, dentistry, and more—but nothing helped.

"If anything," she confessed. "I think she may be getting worse. Especially if she feels any pressure at all."

"What does she do then?" I asked.

"She'll come after you."

We talked a little longer when I asked if I could go in with her, to which Cathy agreed. There have been times when getting information from an owner about a horse with seemingly insurmountable behavior issues, where we find the behavior boils down to some sort of misunderstanding that has put the horse on the defensive. Often, by figuring out what the misunderstanding is and then clearing it up, the horse can be talked off the ledge, so to speak.

I've often said it's not really the horse that is dangerous, but rather the horse's behavior. As humans, we put ourselves in a completely different mindset when we convince ourselves that the animal is dangerous rather than just the behavior. Usually, we feel the need to defend ourselves against a dangerous animal, which sends our nervous system into an aroused state, which can affect our ability to think clearly. Whereas if we can separate the behavior from the animal, we can deal with the behavior at face value, allowing our nervous system to stay in a downregulated state, which then enables us to come into the situation with a clearer mindset.

Going into the pen with the mare, I was hoping a misunderstanding would present itself and we could find a way to begin the process of helping her feel a little better about being around people. Unfortunately, that wasn't to be.

This was the first time in all my years working with horses in which I didn't feel I was working with a horse when I was working with a horse. What I mean by this is whenever we are with horses, no matter how good they are, or even how "bad" they are, we always know we're working with a horse. As prey animals they will almost always act and respond in specific ways in certain situations. In short, even when they have been pushed passed defensiveness into what we might perceive as aggression, they will almost always choose to move away from pressure when enough pressure is applied, especially when there is a way out.

I felt none of that with this mare. I spent about forty-five minutes with her in the pen that day, and the entire time we were together I felt as though I was dealing with a predator. In martial arts, we train extensively to develop skills that allow us to create or find openings in a partner so we can apply techniques. We also train extensively to notice a partner looking for openings in us so they can apply techniques.

The entire time with this mare felt very much like she was waiting for an opening, like she was waiting for my guard to come down so she could get in. As time went on, it ever more increasingly became less about me working toward trying to help the horse and more about making sure I didn't give her an opportunity to do something I'd regret.

It was a zero-sum situation that, after a while, I saw no point in continuing, so I left the pen. Crissi would tell me later that it was the only time she'd ever worried when she watched me work with a horse.

"It looked like you were in that pen with a shark," she said.

As I left the pen, an auditor asked what the best course of action would be for a horse like this.

"Personally," I said after hesitating. "I'd probably put her down."

A noticeable gasp went up from the crowd. I went on to explain that we can think of horse behavior as having parameters. These parameters are quite expansive, and they encompass everything you could think of inherent to how horses act given any variety of situations. I then added it seemed clear what we were seeing from this mare was not even close to being inside those parameters. She had already hurt several people in unprovoked attacks, and given the opportunity, would probably hurt more.

I also pointed out the legal liability of owning, selling, or even giving a horse like the mare away. If someone—a farrier, vet, or just a person passing by—became seriously injured by her, her owners could easily open themselves up for a lawsuit simply because of her known history.

"I've actually been planning to put her down," Cathy added. "But I wanted to bring her here to see if I was missing anything."

It was about then that several auditors began to protest.

"Surely something can be done," someone said.

"She's so pretty, I bet with enough time…." said another.

"Seems a shame just to give up on her."

"Have you tried…?"

It was about here that I interrupted.

"I can't speak for Cathy," I said. "But my guess is, if anybody would like to take this mare home today, she'd probably just give her away."

Things suddenly got very quiet. After several seconds…

"I don't have room at my place," came a reserved voice.

"I couldn't afford to keep her," came another.

"My husband only allows geldings," said still another.

"With the price of hay and all…."

"See, that's the problem," I offered. "Everybody wants to save a horse like this, but nobody wants her in their backyard. And that's fair enough. I wouldn't want her in mine, either. So maybe we can respectfully leave the decision of what to do with her up to the person whose backyard she does live in."

Of the hundreds of horses we've seen over the years with traits and behaviors consistent with inbreeding, we've probably been able to confirm through documentation about two-thirds of them. The rest, like Cathy's horse, may have had all the signs, but because of a lack of lineage documentation, we never could say for sure. Those horses always left me wondering.

Then, some time back, I had a conversation with a friend in the Southwest who hadn't been able to progress much with her unregistered horse's training for about eight years. I asked her about his ability to retain information, which she said he really struggled with, and she said he also struggled with balance issues and seemed to panic in the canter whether being ridden or in the pasture (if he cantered at all). He was also unusually spooky, even in familiar situations and areas.

She also mentioned that when her horse was in with a group of horses that he felt comfortable with, he would be okay. When he was taken out to be worked, he would remain calm for about a half hour, then start slipping right back into his "normal" patterns.

At any rate, this conversation eventually led me to wonder if any scientific evidence existed that might help connect these traits specifically to inbreeding, even though there may not be any lineage documentation to back it up. I decided to check with Dr. Steve Peters to see if he might have some insight. Not surprisingly, he did. The following is part of a conversation Dr. Peters and I had, printed with his permission:

In answer to your question, I found a few small studies that support exactly what you describe in terms of learning, which we can scientifically support by isolating and statistically measuring how significant the variable and degree of inbreeding is on learning potential in horses. No surprise here, increased inbreeding = decreased learning potential.

Here is the conclusion from one well-done study.

"Conclusion: The outcomes of this study showed that there is a significant difference in the learning profile of the three horse breeds investigated. A difference in speed of learning was evident when comparing a domesticated with a wild-type horse species. Domestication as such, however, did not account for these differences. Either the domestication event as such did not have an impact on the cognitive abilities of the horse, or the particular Przewalski horses used in this study had at some point in the past been handled to a greater extent than was known to the current owner. In contrast, the potential impact of inbreeding on learning ability was identified as a significant factor in this study. The only participating breed group with a low inbreeding coefficient included in the study was the Paso Fino group. This group showed a learning speed that was significantly faster than the other two groups. Even at the beginning of the trials, the horses in the Paso group exhibited a clear focus on the task and quickly understood what was required from them in order to receive the food reward. Since multivariate analyses indicated that inbreeding was a 'stand alone' factor in accounting for the variance in speed of learning, this finding supports, although cannot entirely confirm, that inbreeding may have

had an effect on the learning ability of these horses. It is valuable knowledge for breeders that non-inbred horses that show a heterogeneous genetic structure may show better learning abilities, which could reduce time spent on training the horse."

In other words, cognitively, you are better off with heterogeneous genetics (from separate families) than homogeneous (inbreed).

I also found evidence of cerebellar changes and atrophy as an inherited gene mutation in inbred horses that can show up as deficits in coordination, gait, and balance, unsteadiness, lurching, in which the horse would not have confidence in their ability to accurately place their feet.

These are questions that are not always asked as either we are not aware of the problem (ignorance), or do not really want to know the answer.

I have been looking very closely at epigenetics, whereby environmental factors such as good care and training can determine which genes turn on and off and can to some extent modify the degree of a negative genetic susceptibility.

While the information Dr. Peters provided wasn't absolutely conclusive, his last paragraph concerning epigenetics did offer some insight as to a possible reason why there seemed to be such a wide range of severity (or lack thereof) of behaviors in inbred horses. It would make sense that horses like Banjo, a solid, albeit a little quirky at times, saddle horse, could be a product of good handling and training while other inbred horses whose handling and training perhaps wasn't as productive couldn't seem to retain even the simplest of information. It also helped to explain why one inbred horse could be safe enough for kids to ride, while others are so unpredictable you wouldn't even want to be in the same pen with them, and why some remain steady throughout their entire lives while the behavior of others deteriorates over time.

Don't get me wrong here, there's still a lot to be learned about horses with these kinds of issues, and even after all these years it seems as though I'm just scratching the surface with my understanding. Still, it's important for us to accept that sometimes the issues a horse experiences may have very little to do with us, who we are as horse people, or the level of skills we possess. Sometimes it's just who the horse is, or who the horse is destined to be.

As I said at the outset, there was a time when I believed all troubled horses could be rehabilitated. Luckily for us, empirical evidence, science, and the horses themselves have taught us it's not always the case. The good news is, knowing the difference ultimately allows us the opportunity to approach them with deeper understanding, better awareness, and more compassion. I don't know about you, but I can use all that I can get.

INTERNAL ELEMENTS OF HORSEMANSHIP

CHAPTER 10

Watch and Learn

"You can see a lot just by observing."

YOGI BERRA

Not long before we moved from the little house near Walter's place to the new house in the next town over, Walter picked up an older dark red gelding from a family that couldn't afford to keep him anymore. Unlike a lot of the horses he took in, this one seemed like a pretty solid citizen. He was easy to catch, groom, saddle, and ride, and would go from one gait to the next if the rider just thought about it.

The one issue he did have, if you even want to call it that, was he would chew on things—halter ropes, reins, jackets if one was handy. He didn't do this all the time, usually just right after being taken out of his pen to be tacked up, or when he was ridden away from the barn or his pasture mates, or if he was confused about what was being asked of him.

Walter gave him to me to work with, probably because he was by far the easiest horse on the place to get along with and probably because when he would eventually move the horse along, he could tell prospective buyers a twelve-year-old boy had been riding him as a selling point.

For the most part I ignored the chewing behavior, especially at first. But as often happens with that type of thing, I slowly found myself becoming annoyed by it. The ropes he chewed on started to fray where he'd been gnawing on them, and they'd turn green from the leftover grass in his mouth. The same would happen with the leather reins he would get hold of, or anything else he put in his mouth, for that matter.

It wasn't long before I was trying to find ways to stop him from chewing once he picked something up or stop him from picking things up in the first place. Nothing I did helped. I even asked Walter what the best way might be to get him to stop.

"Why not just let him do it," was his answer.

"He's ruining ropes," I protested.

"We have a lot of rope."

"He's got his reins all chewed up."

"We have a lot of reins, too."

"But…"

"Let him chew. Pretty quick he'll spit it out and that'll be that," he said, gray cigarette smoke rolling from his mouth. "The more you stop him, the more he'll want to do it."

Of course, he was right. I grudgingly followed his advice and sure enough, the gelding would pick up a rope or rein, chew it for a while, then drop it, after which he would usually look like he was going to sleep. A few weeks later we moved away, and I never did know what became of the big horse.

Folks who have spent any time around young horses know most are usually "mouthy," to some extent. It seems everything goes in baby's mouth, and this often continues until a horse is three and sometimes four years old. The good news is the majority grow out of the behavior, and it's never much of an issue after that.

There are those, however, that never do seem to grow out of it. We've seen quite a few older horses over the years, much like the red gelding Walter had, who continue the behavior throughout their entire lives. In fact, we currently have a twenty-eight-year-old gelding who will chew on halter ropes whenever he's tied, a behavior he's had since before we purchased him twenty-one years ago.

How these older horses exhibit this behavior is as varied as the horses themselves. Some will chew on anything at any time, while others, like our gelding, only do it when they're tied. Still others only do it when they're being ridden, and of these, some chew only when they're standing still, some do it whether they're standing still or moving, and some only do it when they're being shown something new or when they're under emotional stress.

Some owners of horses with this issue do what Walter suggested to me. They let the horse chew on the item until he or she spits it out, then they just go about their business. Some owners encourage the horse to let the rope or rein go by simply sliding a finger or thumb in the corner of the horse's mouth, while others resort to somewhat harsher methods, such as jerking the rope or rein from the horse's mouth.

A method we have used with some success to help a horse rethink chewing was any time the horse picked up a rein or rope, we would attach a task to it. This meant once the item was in the horse's mouth, we would use it to gently ask them to turn, or follow, or perhaps even back up until they decided to let it go. This was effective with some, but not all.

I have to admit, for a long time, I didn't give much thought as to *why* older horses chew on things. The truth is, other than Walter's red horse, I hadn't really seen much of the behavior during my early days. It was only after I started training for the public, and specifically, after I started doing clinics, that I started to see more of it. Even then, most folks were more interested in getting the behavior to stop than trying to figure out where it was coming from, so that's where most of my focus went.

I'm not sure if it's the result of insight that comes with getting older, but at some point, I realized trying to fix problems like this without understanding the cause is like trying to keep water in a bucket with a hole in the bottom.

Eventually, I started paying more attention to these horses, trying to figure out where the behavior was coming from in the first place. I began to find the one common denominator in many of them was stress. Sometimes the cause of the stress was evident, such as horses not understanding what was being asked of them, or being ridden in an unfortunate manner, or having tack that didn't fit properly, or suffering from some kind of physical problem. Other times the cause of the stress was much more subtle, such as the simple act of being led or just standing tied. In some cases, the horse didn't even appear outwardly stressed at all, giving the impression the behavior was more of a habit than anything stress induced.

We also began to notice horses that were allowed to complete the act of chewing would almost always spit the rein or rope out on their own within just a minute or two after having picked it up. Then, almost right after that, nearly all would show signs of releasing emotional tension such as licking and chewing, yawning, rubbing their face on their front legs, and the like.

I have no way of knowing for sure, but my guess is this release of tension was the thing Walter picked up on with these types of horses, which is why he encouraged me to let the big red horse chew to his heart's content.

"Let him chew," he had said. "Pretty quick he'll spit it out and that'll be that."

Then a while back I was listening to Dr. Peters give a presentation that included the subject of *stereotypies* in horses. Stereotypies are repetitive behaviors, such as cribbing (windsucking), or stall-pacing. He mentioned these kinds of behaviors could be caused by anxiety or even some kind of dysfunction of the central nervous system, which can sometimes be brought on by the horse living in high-stress environments. He also mentioned horses that exhibit these types of stereotypies have been shown to have higher levels of *cortisol*, a stress hormone usually found to be lower in horses without these behaviors.

Not long after that, two things happened within just a couple weeks of each other that really piqued my curiosity regarding all of this. The first came in the form of an email from a friend in California I've known and worked with for over twenty years. In it she asked a question regarding her horse, a twelve-year-old gelding I've known since he was two. Together they were now working their way toward Fourth Level in dressage.

Ever since he was little, the gelding had always been a little on the mouthy side and prone to chew on ropes and such. His owner had noticed that on top of his normal mouthiness, he had, from time to time (and as his workload increased), put his tongue out the side of his mouth, especially to the left. But usually as he got stronger, the issue went away. She mentioned that for about the past four months, and as they worked more on everything needed for Fourth Level, the problem presented itself again. This time, however, the issue hadn't gone away. She tried several different bits, all with mouthpieces designed to be very gentle and provide the greatest tongue relief, but none of them helped.

My friend had ruled out saddle fit, feet, and dental issues, and he was being ridden as softly and correctly as possible. A conscientious and skilled rider, she believed the issue stemmed from the gelding feeling stressed, even though she did everything she could to keep the stress level as low as possible. She even went so far as to contact an animal communicator who confirmed the tongue thing was stress-related. At this point, her concern was, after four months, the issue may also be turning into a habit, and she was hoping to get my thoughts on the situation.

As I read her email, my mind kept drifting back to Dr. Peters' presentation, and the information he gave on stereotypies in horses, the stress-related repetitive behaviors. I began to wonder if the kind of tongue behavior and overall mouthiness my friend's horse was exhibiting was somehow related to more dramatic stereotypies, such as cribbing or pacing a stall.

A couple weeks later, we were doing a clinic in the Midwest. One of our student instructors, Kayla, was there and asked if we could take a look at her gelding, Levi, who was struggling with a difficult-to-pinpoint lameness issue. I had known the thirteen-year-old Levi since he was three when Kayla first started him under saddle. Levi was also one of those horses that never outgrew his mouthiness, even though when he was younger, I told Kayla he probably would.

Levi was relaxed and quiet when Kayla brought him into the arena, and he stayed that way while Kayla, Crissi, and I stood discussing the lameness she'd been seeing. After a while Kayla asked him to trot a circle so we could watch him go. The lameness showed up almost right away, and when it did, Levi began pinning his ears and shaking his head.

After a few laps, we had seen all we needed to see, and Kayla asked him to stop. No sooner did he come to a halt than he reached down, picked up the rope he was attached to and began chewing on it. Kayla mentioned that she had given up trying to stop him from chewing a long time ago, and now for the most part, she just let him do it.

"He always spits it out anyway," she said.

Sure enough, after a minute or so, Levi did just that, then immediately began to yawn. This was not some little mamby-pamby yawn, either. This was a head-twisting, mouth wide open, eyes rolled back in his head kind of yawn where we could almost hear the muscles of his jaw stretching. That yawn was followed by several smaller yawns, which was followed by him rubbing his face on his front leg, which was followed by him licking and chewing, which was followed by him reaching around and scratching his barrel with his teeth, and, finally, looking like he was falling asleep.

It seemed what we just witnessed was a horse who became physically and emotionally stressed (by being asked to move on a sore limb) and then used chewing the rope as the impetus to defuse that stress.

With this coming right on the heels of the email from my friend in California, and with years of my own curiosity about horses with these behaviors now in full swing, I once again reached out to Dr. Steve Peters. My main question for him this time was did he have any thoughts on whether what we were seeing was indeed stress-related, and if so, could this behavior perhaps be a low-level form of cribbing. He kindly answered:

> The research looks at these kinds of behaviors as stress-reducing, coping mechanisms and not necessarily to the point of becoming an addiction such as cribbing.
>
> However, both begin in response to increased cortisol.
>
> Also, the fact that you often see subsequent head-shaking, yawning, and licking and chewing afterward would indicate that it is working, and researchers do see a reduction in cortisol afterward.
>
> This behavior is probably quite reassuring to the horse knowing that they can self-regulate their own stress. Other behaviors in the literature with some similar releases are the face-rubbing on the forelimbs or self-grooming by turning the head and nipping at the side or hind leg.
>
> Because it works and gives these horses a release/relief, the chemical change it creates is putting our horse in a better state (reducing stress). I think if someone were to continually try to correct a horse or take that away from them, they would just increase the cortisol levels.
>
> Funny what we might refer to as a bad behavior in a horse (actually it is a good coping mechanism because it works), we don't see in ourselves (for example, rubbing our sweaty palms on our pants or running our fingers through our

hair, clicking our pen, tapping our feet, chewing our fingernails, and so on to self-soothe our own stress).

For generations, mindful horsemen and women, many with limited means and little formal education, learned about the horse from the horse. They watched and observed. They picked up on patterns, some subtle, some not, but all of which ultimately helped to forge their knowledge. It was knowledge that could be trusted because it came from the source.

I believe Walter was one of these people. Way back when he suggested I let the big red horse chew on his halter rope or his reins, he inherently knew it would help the gelding feel better. This was no doubt based on a lifetime of careful observation, of watching, noticing, and comparing. Yet at the time, I never gave much thought to how he arrived at his conclusions about horses. I was a kid and for the most part, kids just accept the fact that adults know a lot of stuff because, well, they're adults.

It isn't long, however, before even kids begin questioning the information they receive from adults. They become curious beyond what they're told and so the quest for more information begins. This is what happened with me. Walter was able to offer a viable solution to the problem, but over time, just having the solution didn't seem to be enough. That's when the curiosity kicked in.

The same curiosity, I'm sure, that allowed Walter to find the answer for how to best deal with "mouthy" horses, was also the same curiosity that prompted me to wonder what causes the behavior in the first place. There is also a distinct possibility the qualities and skills he used to find his answer were probably the same qualities I ended up using to find mine. I think it says something that, even in this time where all the information in the world is literally at our fingertips, there's still room for learning through simple observation, watching, noticing, and comparing.

I had a brief moment the other day where I wished I could see Walter again and share the information I've learned about these horses. I pictured myself telling him about how research has now shown horses with this particular behavior do it to regulate their stress, and how he'd been right about allowing them to do it as a way to help them feel better.

Then, clear as day, a picture of his reaction suddenly appeared. As I finished talking, he took his cigarettes from his shirt pocket and tapped the top of the pack on the back of his weathered hand. With the flick of his wrist, the end of one of the cigarettes popped from the pack. He put it between his lips, pulling it out the rest of the way, then lit it with his well-worn Zippo lighter. As smoke rolled from his nose and mouth, he nodded, slow and deliberate, like he always did.

"I see," the picture of him said. "Well, we got horses to tend. Best get to it."

CHAPTER 11

Connection

"All things are connected like the blood that unites us.
We do not weave the web of life; we are merely a strand
in it. Whatever we do to the web, we do to ourselves."

CHIEF SEATTLE

I was trying to recall the first time the concept of *connection* in relation to horses showed up on my radar. After a good deal of pondering, I finally realized it wasn't until after I started doing clinics over thirty years ago that I heard anybody even mention it.

Prior to that, my time had been spent either with Walter and his horses, almost all of which were just passing through, or working on and managing ranches where the sheer number of horses offered little time for developing more than a passing rapport with most. The idea of intentionally trying to *connect* with our horses never entered my mind. Probably because nobody I was around ever used the word in relation to horses, or at least nobody I remember.

When I got older and began ranching, there were always certain horses I might choose over others when a job needed to be done. This was usually because I knew that particular horse could help me get the job done. My good saddle horse Buck was one of those. Still, the idea of being *connected* to even those horses wasn't something I gave a whole lot of thought to, if any. I think back then I saw what we had going on with our horses as more of a working relationship or a job-related partnership, if you will.

I can't say for sure if someone mentioned the idea at my very first clinic, but if it wasn't at the first one, it wasn't long after. Not only that, but I'd have to say at least one person in every clinic from then till now has told me developing connection is the number one thing they want to work on with their horse.

Initially, I didn't quite understand the context when people told me they wanted to connect with their horses. I soon began to realize, however, the idea of connection meant different things to different people. For some it meant a physical connection, others wanted an emotional connection, some wanted both, while still others wanted something altogether different.

The one constant in all of this was the folks looking for connection. Their horses, however, almost always had some kind of unwanted training issue going on. These ranged anywhere from the horse not wanting to be caught, to being chronically distracted, to not wanting to leave the barn or a buddy, to having trouble with transitions, to any number of other issues. Most of the time these boiled down to simple misunderstandings between the horse and rider, which, once cleared up, helped the rider feel more connected with the horse. This would certainly make sense seeing as how it's difficult to feel good about horses you can't catch or who would rather be with their buddies back at the barn than you. So, while clearing up misunderstandings seemed to be enough for some, there were others for whom the idea of connection went a little deeper.

Back in the spring of 1998 I was doing a clinic in Southern California. It was one of the last clinics where I was still traveling with my long-time ranch horse Buck. For those who may not know, Buck was given to me by a friend when he was seven years old. My friend was foreman on a cattle operation not far from town and had bought Buck and several other horses the year before from a mutual friend up in Minnesota.

Buck was untrained at the time and consequently turned out in a six-hundred-acre pasture on the ranch until my friend could get around to starting him under saddle. Apparently, Buck proved to be a little difficult to catch, and as a result had taken a backseat on my friend's priority list. After a year of him being turned out without any handling, my friend told me he wanted to get him off the feed bill, and if I could catch him, I could have him.

As it turned out, it took me longer to find the big red horse out on the pasture than it did to catch him, and true to his word, my friend signed Buck's AQHA registration papers over to me. From that day forward, Buck and I were inseparable. He quickly became the most dependable and versatile horse I'd owned and would do anything I asked of him, any time, day or night. In fact, the trophy belt buckle I wear to this day is from the only formal competition Buck and I ever entered, a ranch horse versatility contest in which we ended up taking Reserve High Point. The buckle has his name engraved on it.

At any rate, this clinic in 1998 was the first I would be doing since having surgery on my right shoulder a couple weeks earlier. Other than rehab exercises I'd been given, I was supposed to keep the shoulder in a sling and immobilized for six weeks. Unfortunately, my travel schedule made that difficult, and besides, other than some soreness when I moved my arm in the wrong direction, it actually felt pretty okay.

There was a woman at this clinic named Audrey who said she wanted to develop a better connection with her horse. When I'd asked her on the first day to explain "developing a better connection," she had a difficult time describing exactly what she meant. She said she would give it some thought and see if she could find a way to put it in words.

This was back when I was doing four-day clinics and on the second day, Buck was tied to a hitchrail just outside the arena while I was setting up the PA system. The PA was out of Buck's sight under a raised and covered platform that butted up to the short wall of the arena facing north, and the venue's large tack room to the south. Buck was tied to the hitchrail on the west side of the raised platform. After setting up and testing the PA to make sure it was working properly, I went to get him so we could get the day started.

A number of auditors and most of the riders, including Audrey, were already there that morning, and most of them were sitting in the shade of the platform. As I came around the corner and into Buck's sight, he turned, ears up and nickered.

"Hey, buddy," I said, untying him.

"Does he always do that?" The voice came from the nearby platform. I looked up to see Audrey.

I stroked Buck on his forehead. "Sometimes."

Later that day, we were helping a rider and his horse with flying lead changes. Things had gone well, although from time to time the rider's timing had been a little off, which would cause his horse to change in front but not behind. By the time the session was over, the pair were getting clean changes around seventy percent of the time, which was nice progress from not being able to get them at all when we first began the session.

While waiting for the next horse to come in, one of the auditors asked if Buck and I could demonstrate what clean lead changes looked like. It was a reasonable request that I respectfully declined. Buck was twenty-one years old at the time. We had ridden tens of thousands of miles together working cattle, gathering horses, guiding trail rides, ponying colts, dragging calves to the fire, and doing search and rescue in the high country. Most recently he had traveled at least a half-million miles in the back of my trailer helping me with clinics all over the country. Once the fastest horse I'd ever been on, he was now showing signs of slowing down, including the very first signs of an intermittent mystery lameness numerous vets, chiropractors, and bodyworkers couldn't seem to figure out.

"He's only got so many lead changes left in him," I explained as I petted him on his neck. "I'd rather save them for when we need them, not use them up on demonstrations."

People seemed to understand, and soon enough we moved on to the next horse, a recently gelded two-year-old who was having trouble figuring out how to give to pressure. The youngster was starting to get some size to him and had taken to dragging his owner around by the halter rope instead of yielding when asked.

When I say he was starting to get some size to him, it meant he'd recently gone through a growth spurt where, according to his owner, he'd gone from being under fourteen hands and five hundred pounds to almost fifteen hands and eight hundred pounds. She'd decided if she didn't get a handle on the issue soon, she might not be able to get it under control at all.

Buck and I started slow, asking the gelding to follow us for maybe a step or two, then stop. As it seemed he was starting to feel okay about that, we increased the distance, which he also seemed to feel all right about. Eventually, we were ponying him around the arena. From time to time, he would hang on the halter rope or pull forward trying to pass us, and when he did, I'd take a dally on my saddle horn, letting him pull on the horn rather than me until he'd find a way to give to the pressure and come back.

He seemed to realize relatively quickly that while his 14.3, eight-hundred-pound size was big enough to drag a small woman around, it wasn't quite enough to drag a 15.3, twelve-hundred-pound Buck around. After about thirty minutes, we seemed to be getting a handle on things. He was following nicely, no longer trying to take the slack out of the rope either by pulling or hanging, and appeared to be picking up on the overall concept without any further worry or trouble.

Once he was feeling better about the whole thing, and after having given him several breaks throughout the process so he could give everything a little thought, we started doing a few little exercises to help him follow the feel of the rope to make sure he wasn't just following Buck's body movement while ponying him. We did this with Buck standing still and me guiding the colt around Buck's body with the halter rope.

This was something he was doing pretty well right up until my PA system made a loud popping sound. It would do this from time to time when the transmitter for my mic was starting to lose battery power. The sound surprised the colt who shied, jumping out and around the front of Buck.

This wasn't much of a spook and would no doubt have been brought under control had I been able to take a quick dally around the horn. Unfortunately, the signal from my brain to my arm telling it to move must have been slowed from the recent surgery, and as a result my arm took a more circuitous route to the horn than normal. This awkward movement only served to worry the colt more, resulting in him turning his head and trying to bolt. Luckily, I still had a considerable amount of strength in my hand and was able to hold on to my end of the rope as the colt turned. Not so luckily, I had almost no strength in my shoulder and as the pain exploded through my arm when it extended as far as it was going to go, the rope pulled free of my hand.

This pain caused my arm to instinctively recoil tight against my body, and as it did, Buck took over. He burst forward after the colt as if shot out of a gun. With the colt's halter rope dragging behind him, the youngster zigzagged his way at a dead run to the other end of the arena, head high and looking back over first one shoulder, then the other. Each time his head moved left or right, Buck would effortlessly swap leads accordingly, preparing himself in case the colt decided to go off in that direction.

The whole thing was over in a matter of seconds. The colt, once on the far end of the arena, put himself in one of the corners and having been cut off from running any further by Buck, the youngster stopped. Buck and I eased up to him, I picked up his halter rope, and we continued on with our business as if nothing happened.

When the day was over, Audrey came up while I was pulling Buck's tack.

"I know what kind of connection I'm looking for with my horse," she said.

I placed Buck's saddle on the rack in my trailer. "What kind is that?"

"The kind you have with Buck."

As I said earlier, prior to this time I hadn't thought about relationships between horses and humans in terms of connection. I understand now this was because the idea hadn't been presented to me in that context before. The funny thing is, almost as soon as the idea was brought to my attention, it made perfect sense. This was unlike what happened when people started claiming horses had the ability to understand the concept of respect and disrespect, which never made sense to me, and still doesn't.

It didn't dawn on me that the intangible aspect of what Buck and I had could be considered some sort of transcendental (for lack of a better word) *connection* until Audrey mentioned it.

To say a lot has changed when it comes to my thoughts on connection between horses and humans since those early days would be an understatement. I've gone from virtually no awareness of the concept to what I now feel is a considerably deeper understanding.

This change began with me trying to help riders connect with their horses by clearing up misunderstandings. We could say this was a training-based approach that focused exclusively on trying to build connection through teaching the horse how to properly do their job. There was no question things would usually get better between horse and rider when we did this, but something about it always seemed a bit mechanical to me.

I stayed with this approach for quite a while with varying degrees of success until a series of events took place that forced me to reevaluate my life in general, and my understanding of connection in particular.

Without going into a lot of detail, I'll say this reevaluation began on New Year's Day of 2001 with Buck's unexpected passing and culminated six years later with me trying to navigate my upcoming divorce. In between, I lost my dad, my horse Mouse, three good working dogs, had to deal with a recession that nearly put me out of business, a marriage that was falling apart, and I was slowly being overtaken by the effects of some substantial childhood trauma I'd unsuccessfully attempted to emotionally push aside for decades.

There were times during this period when it felt like I was being pulled along by a slow-moving train headed for a cliff. The worrisome part was I couldn't stop the train and couldn't get myself loose from it.

I did what I could to not let the things occurring in my personal life affect my professional life, and for a while I was successful. But the train kept moving, dragging me along with it and, eventually, my work with horses began to suffer. I can think of at least two occasions (maybe more) during this time when my decision-making was not as good as it could have or should have been, and horses ended up paying the price as a result.

Things finally came to a head as, metaphorically speaking, the train started to nosedive off the cliff. I could feel things unraveling about a week before I was to go to Washington State to do a series of clinics. For some time prior to that trip, I had been seeing someone regarding my childhood trauma. I was told that eventually everything that happened to me, and which I had subconsciously refused to deal with, would come out and when it did, life would get messy.

The therapist was right. As I started to get ready for the trip, I could feel myself internally coming apart, so much so I considered canceling the clinics. Then, at the last minute, I changed my mind, believing I could "will" my way through.

To this day, the experience is surreal to me. I recall getting through the morning of the first day of what was to be the first clinic. All this means is I know I worked riders and horses, but I don't remember who the riders were, the horses we worked with, or what we worked on.

After the morning sessions were over and during our lunch break, something happened. I don't remember exactly what it was. Maybe somebody did something or said something, or maybe I saw something…it's hard to say. Whatever it was, it apparently ended up being the last emotional straw for me because I remember nothing of the afternoon. Nothing at all. In fact, as I write this and try to dredge up some sort of memory of it, all I get is the color white, as if I'm staring at a blank sheet of paper.

Everything else beyond that afternoon is sketchy at best and my memories of the next several days are not clear at all. It's like looking at a painting where the artist only used broad strokes from the brush without filling in any details. I must have canceled all the clinics on that trip, and apparently left the clinic I was doing the following day. The next thing I remember with any clarity is being in the desert in Utah. Everything else for that three- or four-day period is mostly a blur.

This incident, as uncomfortable as all of it was, marked a turning point in my recuperation, and from then on, the worst appeared to be over. I still had some work to do, but from that point forward, I was definitely on the mend. Not only did I start feeling much better emotionally, but I also started to develop a clarity in my work with horses and people that I'm not sure was there previously. One of the elements of my work that benefitted from this change was my appreciation for the idea of connection.

Prior to this I think I may have believed connection with horses was something that could be achieved through training. After this experience, I came to understand while training certainly plays a role, true connection goes much deeper. Specifically, before we can expect to connect with our horse, we should at least make the effort to be connected to ourselves.

Connecting to ourselves may mean different things to different people, but I believe a big part of self-connection boils down to being centered and grounded. I say this as someone who knows what it feels like to be on both sides of that fence, centered and grounded…and not.

There are many paths to achieving a balanced and centered state, and I don't have the market cornered on any of them. With that in mind, however, I would like to offer a few of the more common examples of things we've found that can help improve one's skill at being centered, balanced, and connected.

The first thing I'd like to mention along these lines is developing the ability to see things and situations as they are. We often feel the need to make up stories around what we're experiencing, usually to our emotional detriment. This is especially true when the story we tell ourselves has absolutely nothing to do with what is actually going on, causing us to jump to unrealistic and sometimes troublesome conclusions.

I've offered a few instances in previous chapters of how we make up stories about situations we encounter, not the least of which is us believing horses have the capacity to understand abstract concepts. Something as simple as believing our horse is "intentionally being bad" (when the horse has no concept of good or bad) can easily take us away from being emotionally and physically centered, which in turn can disturb our ability to connect to ourselves.

Another thing that can cause us trouble is the inability to emotionally regulate ourselves throughout the day. For some folks, every situation they experience holds an equal amount of importance, which is often way more than the situation deserves. For example, there are folks out there for whom spilling milk on the kitchen counter might hold the same amount of importance as breaking down on the freeway. This allows for very little in the way of internal balance, and again, interferes with self-connection. Developing the ability to recognize when we're giving something or a situation an undue level of importance can go a long way to helping us recenter and reset our all-important internal balance.

Another thing that gets in the way of centering is when riders get so focused on something unwanted their horses are doing or "thinking," or where their horses are looking, or whatever, that they actually end up feeding into the very behavior they don't want. This usually only serves to create a negative feedback loop between the pair that can be very difficult to break out of.

Still, even this can be overcome by riders simply letting go of what they *don't* want their horses to be doing, focusing on what they *do* want, and then offering their horses direction toward that goal. Doing something as simple as this can, in turn, allow riders to get back in their bodies, center themselves, and ultimately create an internal reconnect.

These are just a few of the more common examples of things we've focused on with riders to help improve their ability to be centered, balanced, and connected. However, in my own quest to better understand connections between horses and riders, I soon discovered one more aspect of the equation.

———

Let's, for a second, think about the kind of connection we're talking about with horses in terms of electricity. If I want the bulb in my lamp to light up, I'll need to first plug the lamp into an electrical outlet. Once attached to the outlet, the lamp can access the electrical current and the bulb lights up. However, the electrical current going to the bulb isn't *just* going to the bulb. Rather, the current also periodically reverses direction away from the bulb, which then allows for a completed circuit all the way back to the source.

I mention this because many riders wanting to connect to their horse often end up with something a little more one-sided. What I mean by that is riders send their intent to the horse, like electricity to the lamp, but they're so focused on sending, they don't give much thought to whether or not the horse is reciprocating. Because they don't wait, or even look for the horse's "current" to come back to them, the circuit is never completed.

This was a stumbling block for me for quite a while. After all, how can there be a connection when there isn't a completed circuit? Not only that, but for the most part, today's humans aren't all that proficient at connecting to others in the first place. Heck, we're not even all that good at being connected to ourselves half the time. On top of that, the society many of us live in not only promotes being disconnected, in many ways, it actively pushes us in that direction.

Just a hundred short years ago, the majority of the United States population was based around small, tightly knit rural communities where horses and livestock were an essential part of life. These were towns and villages where the inhabitants interacted face to face, every day with family, friends, and neighbors, where everyone knew everyone else and where, if someone fell on hard times or needed help, the whole community often pitched in to get them back on their feet.

Today, in contrast, the majority of the population lives in or around major cities and much of our interacting with others is done by staring at various social media platforms through electronic devices for hours at a time, day in and day out.

It's no wonder why some of us find it difficult to connect with our horses. We get good at the things we practice, so if we practice being disconnected all day, every day, chances are we'll get good at it. We also don't get good at things we don't practice, so if we're not good at connecting, we usually won't actively look for ways to get better. Most of the time, we don't even know we're not good at it...until we try.

Okay, so here's the good news. While, in general, we may not be very good at connecting, horses are actually very good at it. It's factory-installed equipment for them. They are so good at connecting, in fact, many is the time where someone might be hauling horse "A" in a trailer, then stop to pick up horse "B." These two horses have never met and are complete strangers, yet, once they arrive at their destination and both are taken out of the trailer, it's as if they've known each other all their lives. In the short time they've been together in that trailer, often without even having had the opportunity to touch noses, they will begin worrying and calling for one another as soon as they are out of each other's sight.

Another example we've all probably seen is where a herd of, say, ten horses are all running together in a pasture. While running, one of them turns and immediately they all turn. This happens as a cohesive unit, not as ten separate horses turning in ten different directions at ten separate times. There aren't any horses in the herd saying, *Okay, everybody, on the count of three we're all turning to the right.* Rather, it just happens through some sort of connection within the herd.

Here's where it gets interesting. We have found whatever it is connecting horses with other horses in these types of situations is the same kind of connection available to us as riders. The catch is, it doesn't happen by us connecting to them, but by us allowing them to connect to us, which is what they want to do anyway.

The way I usually describe what I believe is happening is this: Let's say when we are on our horse there is an imaginary tube that runs from the inside of our horse to the inside of us. Through the inside of the tube is where the energy flows that creates the internal connection we seek with our horse. We'll also say both ends of this tube have removable lids that can be used to open and close on either end.

For argument's sake, we'll say the horse is always trying to send connective energy up through the tube toward us. However, when we decide to connect to our horse, we start sending energy down the tube toward them. When this happens, our two energies collide somewhere inside the tube with neither energy ultimately reaching its destination. The result is a lack of internal flow between us and our horse, which then causes us to have to rely exclusively on physical aids to communicate with them. This is because our internal connection, the part that allows our horse to access our intent, isn't available. By the way, the same thing can occur when we intentionally close off the opening on our end of the tube. This can happen when all we really want from our horse are results without much concern of how the horse feels about it. In a case like that, the horse usually tries to reach us through the tube, but because we've closed off our end, they are unable to get to us. In worst-case scenarios, the horse might give up trying to connect altogether and ultimately close off their end of the tube as well, leaving us not much to work with at all.

Don't get me wrong, using physical aids to communicate is certainly not a bad thing, especially when done with the right intent. In many cases, physical aids are what is needed, particularly in the early stages of a relationship with a horse when we're trying to get on the same page with them. But if we're looking for a deeper relationship with our horse where physical aids can be transcended, we must look beyond the physical and turn more inward.

At this point, I'd like to add a couple pieces to the equation that may be helpful. The first is, as I've mentioned, in general humans are not very good at connecting. Horses, on the other hand, are very good at it. Horses are also very good at finding openings. They can find openings in fences, in a rider's intent, in someone's lack of direction or judgment.

On the other side of the coin, humans are very good at creating openings. In fact, we're so good at it we often create them even when we don't know we're doing it. Something else we're very good at as humans is directing—telling others where to go and what to do.

So, to recap, humans are good at creating openings and directing. Horses are good at finding openings and connecting.

With these factors in mind, we've found a sort of roadmap that can help in successfully developing connection with horses. The basic idea is for both us and our horse to play to our strengths. It begins with us creating an opening for the horse. The horse finds the opening, goes through the "tube," and connects. Then we direct.

Here's an example of what this might look like in real life. Let's say we're riding along, and we'd like to go from our walk to our trot. Rather than first applying leg to get the transition, instead we feel the rhythm of the trot we're looking for in our body. This is not a physical thing we do, but instead it's all internal. We could even think about it in terms of what it would *feel* like if we were on the ground without our horse, and we wanted to go from a walk to a jog. We need to ask ourselves what the *internal* process in us is when we set up to do *our* transition. That is the same feel we offer our horse when we ask for our walk-trot transition.

By doing this we create an opening for the trot by putting the feel of the trot in our body. The horse finds the opening and connects to the trot. At this point, we will almost always feel some sort of effort on the horse's part to move to the trot. Sometimes, they'll effortlessly go to the trot. Other times, they may offer a subtle change of speed, a flick of an ear, a change in the way they're breathing, or sometimes, they may even glance back in our direction. Either way, we have created an opening, the horse has found the opening and connected to what we are offering. Finally, if we need to, we can offer direction by applying a little leg.

Even if the horse doesn't immediately go to the trot, which many don't, especially if all they know are mechanical cues, all we need to do is stay connected to ourselves (using some of the elements I referred to earlier), stay focused on the task, and back up our intent with physical aids if needed. Before long, if we are consistent and persistent, our horse will almost always begin responding to our intent and the physical aids can then drop away.

Many are the riders from all over the world who have told me how they were just thinking about doing something while riding their horses, and suddenly their horses just did it without being asked. I believe this is a result of the riders having allowed, perhaps unwittingly, their horses to connect to them, and the horses, in turn, responding to the riders' intent.

At the outset, I mentioned how, back in the day, I didn't quite understand the context when people first told me they wanted to connect to their horses. I also mentioned how the word "connection" meant different things to different people. I still think it means different things to different people, and there's certainly no harm in that.

I do think, like most things when it comes to horses and horsemanship, we need to look at ideas and concepts we are presented with, figure out what they mean to us, then work toward shaping them in a way that best suits our own horsemanship.

To that end, while the concept of connection in relation to horses may have been foreign to me at first, I believe the underlying philosophy behind the idea (as I understand it today) has always been with me. I say this because my overall goal has almost always been for my horses to be able to function as easily with me on their back as they can when they're out in the field by themselves. Now, as a result, when someone asks me how I define connection in relation to horses, I usually just say I think of it as effortlessness in communication resulting in an effortlessness in movement.

As goals go, I'm thinking that's not such a bad one to have.

CHAPTER 12

A Shift of Perspective

"I do not fix problems. I fix my thinking.
Then problems fix themselves."

LOUISE HAY

This is probably going to sound a little funny, but until the mid-1980s I never as-sociated the word "technique" with working with horses. To me, working with horses had always just been *working with horses.*

Then, while working at the big dude outfit, the boss bought a pair of young Belgian draft horses he wanted to get going in harness and asked if I wanted to help out. I was one of the only wranglers with experience as a teamster at the time, and, in fact, had been driving one of the ranch's two working teams for the nightly hayrides all sum-mer long. The boss drove the other. With the summer season winding down and my evenings free, I told him I'd be happy to give him a hand.

As it turned out, the youngsters weren't completely green. They apparently had about thirty days of experience pulling a variety of horse-drawn equipment on a ranch up north somewhere. Because they had some experience, I assumed the boss would want to hook each of them with one of his experienced draft horses to continue their education and get them used to pulling in the new environment. I figured after the youngsters felt good about working alongside the older horses, the next natural step would be to hook them together.

Instead, the boss decided he wanted to start the young team out by ground driving them around the property. He mostly wanted me there as a sort of outrider, walking alongside the team's heads to help calm them if they started to worry. So that's what we did. He drove, I walked slightly ahead and just to the side of the left-hand horse. By doing this I was making sure the youngster could see me, unobstructed by the blinders he was wearing.

After a while, I moved to the other side and took up the same position slightly ahead of and just to the side of the right-hand horse. After about an hour without incident, we put the team up, bringing them out the next evening and doing the same thing.

It became clear within about fifteen or twenty minutes of our second outing that the pair was fine. If you didn't know any different, you'd think they were a couple of old hands that'd been there and done that. To make sure they weren't just being quiet because they were following me, I eventually dropped back out of their sight. No change.

Up till this point, and other than not actually being hooked to anything and pulling weight, the only thing missing was noises from behind. Of course, the boss would talk to them as they were being driven, but in general the area we were working had been pretty quiet, so we didn't know if they were going to be reactive to unexpected noises or sounds.

I mentioned this to the boss and asked if he wanted me to find a way to get a little noise going from behind, and he agreed. I eventually found six-foot-long, two-inch diameter metal pipe just off the gravel road we were on. Walking along behind the boss, I began by dragging the end of the pipe on the gravel for a couple seconds at a time, watching the horses closely as I did.

They jumped a little the first couple of times they heard the rattle of the pipe, but quickly settled down after that. Before long, and by slowly increasing the length of time I made noise with the pipe, I could continually drag the pipe, drop it, toss it on the ground, or whatever without them so much as flinching.

After we'd finished up and were pulling the horses' harness, the boss looked over at me.

"Where'd you learn that little technique?" he asked.

'Technique?"

"Yeah, the pipe thing."

"We wanted some noise, so I used the pipe."

This little exchange epitomizes my understanding of "technique" regarding horses at the time. With Walter, we never had any special tools or tack or whatever. If a tool was needed but not available, we just used whatever was handy to get the job done. If we needed to lead a horse from point A to point B and didn't have a halter or rope, a belt or shoelaces or baling twine would work just as well. In this case, we needed some noise, and a pipe was as good a tool as any.

The part I was missing was my boss wasn't referring to the pipe itself as the technique. He was referring to how I *used* the pipe. Offering noise, a little at a time, increasing the intensity of sound and length of time only as the horses became accustomed to it, *that* was the technique part. Just like using a belt or shoelaces or baling twine to lead a horse isn't a technique. How you get them to move using those things is the technique.

In other words, technique isn't *what* you use, it's *how* you use it. Or, at least, that's how I have come to understand it. Perhaps another way to say it is *we* are the technique. To that end, if we want to improve our technique, we'll also need to improve ourselves. It's been my experience the more we focus on our own self-improvement, the less external tools we need in the first place.

Not everybody sees it that way. For some, specific techniques are often connected to certain tools, such as flags, whips, sticks, spurs, tie downs, side reins, and so on. What I mean by this is some folks get so married to their tools, they (and their horses) can get a little lost without them.

We've seen quite a few horses over the years that load into a trailer perfectly fine as long as owners have a flag in their hand but won't load at all when the flag isn't there. We've seen horses that would lunge like nobody's business when the owner held a whip, but barely moved without the whip. We've seen lots of horses that were extremely responsive as long as the rider wore spurs, but were completely the opposite when the spurs were removed. The same goes for horses ridden in leverage bits. If the rider had one in the horse's mouth, the horse would do anything the rider asked. Without the leverage, the horse would suddenly forget how to respond to the rider's hands.

I expect there are folks out there who would say the horses I just mentioned were trained with those tools so responding to the tool is all they know. Furthermore, it's unfair to the horse to remove the tool and expect the horse to respond as if the tool was still there. I wouldn't disagree with that. But in a way I think the argument proves the point that the technique is tied to the tool (external) rather than it being tied to the person (internal).

When it comes to the idea of technique, I've noticed over the years there are more or less four kinds of riders.

There are those who rely solely on external technique and don't care all that much about the internal aspects of riding. This type of rider can be seen to some extent in almost every corner of the horse world, from simple trail riding to ranch work to top-level show rings and beyond.

Along these same lines, there are riders who rely solely on external technique but *say* they are working internally. I believe many of these folks have been introduced to a different, perhaps more mindful way of being with their horse but haven't quite gotten a handle on what that is or what it really means to them—yet.

Then there are riders who bounce back and forth between internal and external technique. They focus on handling or riding their horse internally in one situation, such as an activity the horse is used to and feels good about, but then switch to riding externally in situations where the horse isn't as settled. These folks usually have some foundation on internal aspects of riding, but because of limited practical experience, are forced to fall back on the external aspects when things get a little hairy.

Finally, there are the riders who focus almost exclusively on the internal aspects of technique.

Before we discuss these internal aspects, I'd like to mention all these descriptions are based simply on observations and not meant as a judgment toward anybody. The truth of the matter is, most riders, regardless of current skill level, have undoubtedly passed through, or will pass through, one or more of these levels at one time or another anyway. Of course, this is provided they are actively trying to keep improving their education, which, truthfully, some aren't all that interested in.

I see folks who choose not to continue the learning process as being quite like what is often seen with some students in a martial arts *dojo*. The students begin training and eventually start moving up in rank. Maybe within a few years they've been promoted to a level somewhere in the middle of the ranking system. It's clear the students have talent which, over time, would certainly translate into increased understanding and skill development within the art. Yet, for whatever reason, they become satisfied with the stage they've reached and choose to discontinue their learning. As a result, their knowledge and skill development, having reached a specific level, effectively comes to an end.

From then on, and regardless of the kind of situation they are presented with in the future, the maximum level of response available to them is limited to the last thing they learned on the day they discontinued their education.

Another way to say this same thing would be the way a riding student put it to me many years ago. Back in the early days of doing clinics, a rider named Jo came into the arena. As is often the case with individuals I haven't worked with before, I asked her how much riding experience she had. She told me she had twenty years of experience.

We worked together over the next four days, and she and her horse made some really nice progress. When the last day of the clinic was over and the riders were loading their horses to go home, Jo came up to me.

"Remember on the first day you asked how much riding experience I had, and I told you twenty years?"

"Yes."

"Well," she continued. "I realize after these four days that's not quite accurate."

"Oh?"

"Yeah. What I really had is one year of experience twenty times."

I don't want people thinking I'm somehow averse to learning external technique. I'm not. Developing good, sound mechanics is extremely important regardless of whether we're talking horsemanship, bowling, driving a car, playing an instrument, or whatever. Physical mechanics are the foundation on which everything else is built. Heck, for well over a decade, every aikido class I ever attended began with at least thirty to forty-five minutes of practicing nothing but foundational techniques.

Having repeatedly witnessed the effectiveness of subtlety in working with horses at such an early age, I was left with an indelible mark on my understanding of what is possible *beyond* external technique. Like my aikido instructor, this mark (unknowingly at first, consciously later) set me on a path of finding ways to transcend the physical technique without abandoning it entirely.

I'm not sure how many stages I've gone through on this search, but I know it's been a lot. Initially, I relied on a shotgun approach, trying almost anything and everything in an attempt at stumbling on the secret. Some things stuck during this period, some didn't. Eventually, I settled on the idea of external physical softness, putting added focus on improving feel, timing, and balance, soft hands and legs, a quiet and balanced seat, and the like.

During this time, I began physically taking better care of myself. I started getting regular chiropractic care and bodywork. I worked out regularly on top of my martial arts training. I ate better and stopped drinking alcohol. All these things made a positive difference in the way I felt, which, in turn, allowed more conscious control over how my body responded when a response was needed.

These efforts definitely paid off because things got progressively better, and I felt as though I was steadily moving toward the kind of subtle communication with horses I had observed when I was younger. But over time, and not unexpectedly I suppose, I slowly found myself hitting a proverbial wall, and progress toward my goal leveled off.

Plateaus in learning are never unexpected and, in fact, are part of the process, so I wasn't too concerned when I first realized it was happening. After a few years of stagnation, however, I knew it was time for a change. The questions was, what kind of change?

About this time, a couple seemingly unrelated things occurred. The first was the *dojo* where I'd been training and teaching for almost two decades moved from our longtime location on one end of town to a new location across town. For some reason, attendance for our aikido classes suddenly dropped to just one or two students. That meant the aikido classes at the *dojo* were canceled altogether, and the remaining students were absorbed into the ongoing karate classes.

I attended these classes both as instructor and student for a time whenever I was in town, but slowly found the competitive nature of some of the karate students, while excellent practice for my aikido training (you find out pretty quickly if your techniques actually work when someone *really* wants to hit or kick you) to be out of line with my overall goal of developing subtle communication with horses. As a result, I gradually found myself stepping away from these classes.

About this same time, Crissi and I began attending classes at another aikido *dojo* about forty-five miles away taught by Ikeda Sensei. These specific classes focused entirely on the internal aspects of aikido rather than external technique, and it didn't take long for me to realize what he was offering was exactly what I was looking for in my quest to understand subtle communication.

Sensei offered exercise after exercise in these classes on ways to better develop center, internal connection (both to us and our partners) softness, balance, and power. After just a few classes I was finding ways of incorporating these ideas directly into my horsemanship, and the results were substantial and immediate.

I very quickly realized by focusing almost solely on external physical softness, I had missed quite possibly the most important part of the equation. Put simply, softness doesn't come from the outside of us. It comes from the inside. In other words, focusing on having soft hands when riding is great, but ultimately it doesn't matter how soft our hands are if the inside of us is as tight as Dick's hatband.

Almost overnight, I shifted my focus from external physical softness to developing my own internal softness. I worked at applying this across the board with every horse I came in contact with and had almost universal positive results. A year or two after Crissi and I began training regularly with Sensei, an example of the kind of results I'd been seeing showed up, and when it did, it was in a very public setting—the Minnesota Horse Fair. More about that in a minute.

In the mid to late 1980s, I was twenty years removed from my time with Walter, and my skill development with horses in the interim had been spotty at best.

This was also the period when I was working on the large dude operation and where the boss wasn't too keen for us to be working with the horses outside business hours. As a result, while I spent a good deal of time in the saddle and with incidental handling of the horses on the place, I wasn't doing a whole lot of formal "training."

In the off seasons, I spent time with my buddy on the cattle ranch he managed, working horses and cattle, and I helped local folks with their horses whenever I was asked. The foundation I gleaned from Walter was extremely helpful during this time, although there were a lot of holes in my education for sure. Because of that, whenever I did help someone with a horse, I usually did it for free. I didn't feel good about charging people for the work I was doing when I was using their horses to further my own education.

Also in the 1980s, the horse industry started seeing an influx of horse training "programs" put together by various trainers. Many of these programs, or at least the ones I was introduced to, touted a sort of one-size-fits-all approach to horse training, with the basic premise of most being: if you do A, the horse will *always* do B.

One of the wranglers I worked with at the dude ranch had bought some videos from one of these training programs, and she offered to share them with the rest of us one evening. This was way before platforms like YouTube were available, and even before computers were a thing. So, before we could watch the videos, we needed to get a VCR machine, program it, somehow get it hooked up to a TV (no small feat back then) and hope the video tape didn't have a glitch in it that would get it bound up inside the VCR, shutting the whole thing down and making it near impossible to retrieve the video.

Several of us sat down and watched the videos. In one of them, I was introduced to a concept I'd never heard before.

Before going any further, I'd like to point out horses are relatively predictable creatures. For instance, if we put one that doesn't want to be caught in a round pen and let them run around a bit, before long they'll find a way to stop, especially if we aren't putting any undue pressure on them. Take a couple steps back when the horse does stop, and chances are they'll turn to look at us. If we add a couple little movements in the right direction at the right time while the horse is looking at us, they'll more than likely come right up to us.

To the untrained eye, or a novice horse person, this seems like magic. It's not. What we're witnessing is the horse's nature in action. Because of the horse's false-positive bias (anything that doesn't look, sound, or smell right is a potential threat) they will initially run from anything that worries them. If a human trying to catch or approach them is a worry, they'll naturally try to get away. This is a fear-based response.

In the wild, a fleeing horse in a panicked state can run at top speed for about a quarter-mile before they would begin to lose steam. In addition, a quarter-mile would be about as far as they would need to go before they outran most predators. The round pen technique I described is loosely based on this idea.

There are lots of reasons why horses might not want to be caught, but with this particular technique, the reason almost doesn't matter. Working with them in the above manner, or something similar, will almost always achieve the same result. This is because once the horse is convinced the human poses no threat, they'll stop trying to get away. At that point, their fear begins to turn into curiosity, which can be helped along by offering a few simple movements on our part that both decrease any pressure the horse might be feeling while at the same time helping to add to their curiosity.

A horse's behavior in this type of situation is so predictable, researchers in Europe were recently able to elicit the same responses from horses in round pens using a small remote-control car as a motivator instead of a human.

I was first introduced to this idea back with Walter when I saw him do something similar with horses that, for whatever reason, weren't interested in being caught. As with most things he did with horses, there was seldom a lot of energy being used on his part in his version of the process.

As I started branching out on my own, I found myself replicating what I saw him do whenever I was presented with a horse that was difficult to catch. Initially, like Walter, I used as little energy or pressure as possible, and for the most part could be successful in helping the horse feel better about being caught. It was for this reason I was quite interested to find one of the videos we watched deal specifically with hard-to-catch horses using what initially appeared to be the same premise.

In the video, the trainer had a gelding in a round pen who kept moving away from him any time the trainer approached. After a few minutes the trainer stopped and faced the camera.

"As you can see," he said. "There isn't enough motivation here for this horse to even try. So, what we're going to do is make the wrong thing difficult and the right thing easy."

Wait. What? I thought to myself. *The wrong thing difficult and the right thing easy? What does that mean?*

With that, he tossed the loop of the lariat he'd been carrying at the horse's hindquarters. The gelding jumped to life and galloped around the pen. For the next several minutes the trainer kept tossing the rope at the horse and the horse kept running.

"He wants to move, which is not what I want," the voice cracked through the speakers on the TV. "So, I'll make him move more."

After quite a few fast and worried laps, the gelding suddenly slid to a stop and turned toward the trainer, head high, eyes wide. The trainer stopped tossing the rope and backed up several paces.

"That's better," he said as the gelding let out a couple loud snorts. "So, I'll make it easy by not chasing him."

Then the gelding, half prancing, half walking, began to approach. He quickly closed the distance by half before wheeling and running off again. The trainer returned to tossing the rope. While moving the horse around, he kept saying he was looking for the smallest "try" in the horse that told him the horse wanted to stop.

It's hard to say for sure due to how grainy the picture on the TV was, but I thought I noticed the horse offer to stop on several occasions. The trainer kept pushing him anyway. This continued for a while until the horse finally veered toward the trainer and trotted up to him, sides heaving, sweat dripping from his belly.

"There," the trainer said. "That's making the wrong thing difficult and the right thing easy."

The Minnesota Horse Fair was held in April the year I first attended the venue. I was scheduled to give a few talks and horse-related demos over the weekend, although due to a recent outbreak of EHV-1 (one form of the highly contagious equine herpesvirus) in Minnesota and Wisconsin, most horses ended up being banned from the event.

Not all was lost, though. A respectable crowd still showed up, one of the horses I was supposed to use for a demo was excluded from the ban and had made it to the show, and an old friend from the area, Lloyd Alm and his family, stopped by to say hello.

Lloyd was a lifelong horseman in his early eighties at the time. He was recovering from a hip replacement that he said was slowing him down from getting much riding in. He'd hoped to heal up fast because he had a couple colts he wanted to get started.

A mutual friend introduced Lloyd and me years before and not only had we become friends, but I also ended up buying a number of good saddle horses from him. In addition, I bought an AQHA foundation stallion and a handful of broodmares from him to use in our breeding program back when we were still raising our own colts. My ranch horse Buck came from Lloyd, as did my longtime clinic horse Rocky. To say he raised good horses would be an understatement.

Lloyd and his family stopped by my booth on Sunday not long before I was to start what would turn out to be my one and only demo. Lloyd's arrival gave us an opportunity to catch up, take a few photos together, and talk horses. Before long, he told me he had to start heading for the coliseum for my clinic because, with his bum hip and all, it was going to take him a little extra time to get there.

I had not met the mare I was to work with that day, although I had met the owner. He was a nice fella with a little horse operation nearby, and he told me the mare I would work with was a very nice little horse that he'd sold to a woman as a trail horse a year or so before. For whatever reason, the woman and the mare didn't get along and after a while he ended up taking her back. When he got her home, she apparently had a few issues, including being a bit pushy and hard to catch.

I showed up about fifteen minutes early, just as the grounds crew was finishing setting up the round pen in the middle of the arena. The demo was the last scheduled event of the expo, and being Sunday, a lot of the attendees had already left for home, trying to get out ahead of a spring storm that was supposed to come in later that evening.

As the tractor that brought the panels in for the round pen left the building, the mare I was to work with was brought through the same gate. She was a little thing, not more than about fourteen hands, well put together, pretty, and not at all happy to be there. She screamed, bucked in place, kicked out with her hind feet, reared, snorted, charged circles around her handler, and screamed some more.

It took a little doing to get her to the round pen, as the sight and sounds of the place seemed all but unbearable to her. Once in the pen, her screaming and behavior intensified. She ran furiously, crashing into the panels, bucking mindlessly, tossing her head so hard she almost took herself off her own feet.

The owner came up to me as they were introducing me over the loudspeaker.

"Could you let the crowd know she's for sale?" There wasn't even a hint of sarcasm in his voice.

"I will," I replied.

The kind applause I received from the crowd did nothing to calm the little mare, who escalated her behavior even more, which almost seemed impossible.

As I reached the pen, I thanked the crowd for the warm welcome, then, fulfilling the owner's request, mentioned the mare was for sale. Brief but not unexpected laughter filled the arena, and as it quieted, I explained what we would be doing to try to help the horse.

"Things haven't gone very well for her this past year," I said, my voice echoing through expansive, half-filled space. "And she hasn't been to town much, so it seems she's feeling a little overwhelmed."

I went on to explain not only was she in a panic, but she seemed to be reaching a point where she couldn't see a way to save herself, which is never a good place for a horse to be. My goal when I went in the pen would be to try *not* to throw any more gasoline on the fire, but rather give her a little direction when an opening appeared and see if that might be enough to get her to reengage with her situation. If we could get her reengaged, she might be able to start looking for a solution to her problem. If we could do that, she might be able to look to me for help, and if that happened, and she could actually see me as a source of help, she might start feeling better.

"Because she sure doesn't like the way she feels right now."

I said this as I placed the halter and rope in the crook of my arm and went in the pen.

For over four years prior to this, I had been focusing almost exclusively on ways to better develop centeredness, internal connection, softness, balance, grounding, and power. For twenty years before that I'd trained in aikido as an avenue to help move my horsemanship forward, and for some forty-six years before that I had been con-tinually searching for better ways of developing subtle communication with horses.

During all that time I found one element critical for success: the way I live my life must mirror my goals. Any time I internally or externally strayed from my path, things seldom went well. Another way to say this is I found I needed to *live* the things I wanted to achieve with horses. These things had to be in me *all the time*, not just when it was convenient.

So, by the time I went into the pen with the mare, I had a pretty good idea when I was "living what I was looking for," and I knew when I wasn't. On this day, I was living what I was looking for.

I entered the pen with the clear intention I was there to help. I also entered with a vivid picture as to what I felt the end result between us was going to be, which was both of us quiet and calm. Beyond that, I would take what she could give.

The mare was still mindlessly stampeding around the pen when I went in, so I went to the middle to see if my presence would have any effect. It didn't, so as she passed a certain point in the pen, I walked directly to that point so by the time she came around again, I was standing in her way.

She skidded to a stop, spun toward the fence, and charged off in the other direction. As she passed another point in the pen, I walked toward it so again, by the time she came around, I was in her way. We did this four or five times before she went from a panicked run to a slower, although not yet relaxed, canter. When she changed speeds, I went back to the middle of the pen to see what she might do next.

She sped up and slowed down a few times, but overall looked as though she was trying to get a handle on herself. After another few laps, she began offering a few quick glances in my direction, and when she did, I would counter with slight movement of my own. Sometimes, this was a small step in one direction or another, other times it was little more than a shift of weight, but everything I did was meant to help divert her attention off her worry and on to my movement.

I want to be clear that I wasn't trying to get her attention *on me*. I was hoping to turn her attention to *the movement I made*. This is why the movement I was making was so small. Small movement in situations like the one with the mare could influ-ence curiosity while big movement often fed into worry. Several times when I offered this movement, the horse would counter with a change of direction, and each time she did, she slowed even more. After a few minutes, it started to become clear she was looking for a way to get herself stopped. The kink in her tail was gone, her head was starting to come down, and she had begun to breathe with a rhythm, whereas just a few minutes before she'd been hardly breathing at all.

I explained everything I was doing to the crowd, and just as I mentioned it was feeling to me like she was wanting to get herself stopped, almost on cue she went from her canter to a trot to a walk and finally she stopped. Many in the crowd responded by applauding, sending her back up into a worried lope, which only lasted a few laps before she slowed herself again. This time I asked for the crowd to refrain from clapping to allow her to settle.

Instead of stopping, she turned herself off the fence, head down, eyes quiet, and made her way up to me. She got to within about arm's length and then stopped. This is usually where most folks would want to reach out and pet a horse that's been struggling a bit. I don't, for a couple reasons.

The first is, for some troubled horses in situations like this, just approaching the person for the first time can be right at the edge of their comfort level. Reaching to pet them can, and often does, send them over that edge and causes them to want to leave. Even if they do stay, they may be *feeling* like they want to go, which is not the mindset I'd like them to have.

The second reason, particularly in this case, was that I was hoping the mare would seek out physical contact, rather than me initiating it. If she would seek contact, as she did a few minutes later, then I knew her nervous system had leveled out enough that she was ready for it.

"I'd like to give her a minute here," I said over the mic. "So, we won't ask anything of her for a bit and let her catch her breath."

I recapped what we'd done with her to this point for the crowd, and after maybe a minute or two, she began a period of licking, chewing, and yawning that lasted quite a while. I was hoping to let her relax more without me standing right next to her, so I slowly started moving away from her.

I moved several feet, far enough to where I figured she wouldn't follow, then turned and walked away, taking up a position near the fence as I continued the recap. I glanced at the mare from time to time. She was standing near the middle of the pen, head down, eyes half closed. A minute or two later, she turned, looked at me, then came over and stood with me.

I haltered her up, mentioning to the crowd that one of the issues she was having was understanding what her boundaries were around people. I told those watching that as long as she was in a little calmer state of mind, we'd go ahead and spend a little time clearing up that misunderstanding.

For the next five minutes or so we worked on helping her recognize where she should be in relation to people whenever she was being led or even if we were just standing together. She quickly picked up on everything I offered, and she seemed quite amenable almost right away.

At this point, about fifteen minutes had gone by since we first started, and there was still over an hour left in the demo. I noticed spectators starting to file out of the arena and having accomplished everything we had set out to do, I spent the rest of the time just leading her around, both inside and outside the round pen. As we got closer to the one-hour mark in the demo, I asked the crowd to clap from time to time to help her feel a little better about the noise that had worried her so much when we first started working with her. After four or five times of applause, she was fine with that as well. With the mare settled, responsive and quiet, and even though we still had a good twenty minutes left, I announced we were done for the day. The owner came in to get her, and with applause from the crowd echoing throughout the cavernous space, she calmly followed him from the arena.

Just outside the arena, I once again ran into Lloyd and his family, and we spent a little longer visiting. After several minutes, Lloyd said they'd better get going as they had a couple-hour drive to get home. We said our goodbyes, and they started to leave. They'd only gone a short distance when Lloyd stopped and turned around.

"You did a nice job with that horse," he said with a slight nod.

It was one of the nicest compliments I've ever received, especially coming from a horseman like Lloyd.

A few minutes later I was back at the booth. A lot of folks were already there, waiting. Some were hoping to get their books signed, some had just stopped by to say hello, and others wanted to tell me stories about their horses.

Several people stood at the table I was using for book signings when a middle-aged man in a cowboy hat and jean jacket slipped in between those standing near the table and pushed his way to the front.

"That was the most boring demonstration I've ever seen," he said, pointing in the direction of the coliseum. "A complete waste of time."

"I didn't think it was," the woman standing next to him said.

"That horse should'a been pushed till her lungs were burning," he growled.

That must have been all he wanted to say because even before he'd gotten those last words out, he'd already turned and was gone. I finished signing the book in front of me and handed it to its owner, a no-nonsense looking woman in clean but well-worn jeans, boots, shirt, and faded barn jacket.

"I'm okay with boring," I shrugged.

"You got that right," she replied, placing the book in a shopping bag filled with newly purchased items from the expo. "I'll take boring any day."

About a year before that Minnesota expo, someone had given us a book called *Beyond Horse Massage* by Jim Masterson, founder of the Masterson Method® Integrated Equine Performance Bodywork. The book was a step-by-step guide for alleviating body tension in horses, and Crissi had been using the information in it on some of our horses.

As it turned out, Jim was also presenting in Minnesota, and on the morning of the first day before the expo opened, Crissi and I went to his booth to introduce ourselves. We got a chance to visit on several occasions over the weekend, and Jim and I found a lot of similarities in our overall goals with horses. The similarities were so close, in fact, Crissi likes to say that Jim was the only other horse professional she'd ever heard, other than myself, say, "When in doubt, go softer."

It became clear through our discussions what Jim was doing with his bodywork was the same thing I was trying to accomplish through training. We were trying to find ways to help the horse release physical and emotional tension, especially when that tension was causing potential communication issues between the horse and human. Not only that, but we were also focusing on the refinement of ourselves and how we presented information to the horse as the incentive for the aiding of that change.

Crissi and I were both quite interested in finding out more about what Jim was doing, so by the time the expo was over, Crissi had booked us in a two-day introductory course with Jim, as well a five-day advanced course, both of which would happen during the upcoming summer.

The benefits of completing both courses were immeasurable for both Crissi and me. Not only did we strike up a long-lasting friendship with Jim, which would eventually translate into us doing clinics together, but Crissi and I both became trained equine bodyworkers, and Crissi went on to become certified in Jim's method.

For me, working with Jim allowed me the opportunity to develop an even deeper understanding of functional anatomy, which, in turn, aided me in the broader understanding of the internal elements of communication. This has helped greatly in the refinement of my requests and, thus, the refinement of the horse's responses.

For instance, rather than initially asking a horse that pushes on the bit to mechanically lower their head or let go of tension in their jaw, I might, instead, target the convergence of neck muscles just behind the pole for softening. This group of muscles is more or less over the top of the second cervical vertebrae and is where three relatively large muscles that help operate the front legs and movement of the head and neck all come together.

These (and all) muscles can only fire or not fire, and clearly a horse pushing on the bit is firing those muscles. Still, the fact the muscles are being fired is not the issue. The intensity at which they are being fired is. The horse has learned to defend against the pressure so the intensity of energy in the muscle is, say, at an "8" or "9" on a scale from "0" to "10." In cases like this, the reason the muscle is firing at that intensity is because the horse, in their original searches to get the pressure to release, no doubt tried to relax the muscle, but when they did, no release came. In fact, the rider, not feeling the horse's attempt at releasing (because of the subtlety of the try), probably pulled right through the attempt, causing the horse to become even more defensive and braced. At this point, the horse is now convinced releasing is not safe, so they defend themselves at an "8" or "9" any time they feel pressure.

To start the process of reversing this, we apply pressure, feeling for the muscle groups I mentioned. At some point, usually after the horse has tried other options to get the pressure to release, such as pushing harder, or raising or tossing their head, they will almost always ever-so-slightly decrease the intensity in those muscle groups. If we aren't soft in ourselves inside and out, chances are we'll never feel the softening of the muscle because it happens on such a subtle level.

Yet, if we feel the decrease in intensity (from a "9" to an "8.75") that also means the horse felt a corresponding release in pressure. The release in pressure, as subtle as it was, gives the horse a shot of dopamine that allows them the confidence to search for that same kind of release the next time they feel pressure. This not only begins the process of reversing the extreme level intensity being used in those muscles, but it also begins to restore the horse's feeling of safety around trying to decrease the intensity in the first place.

Slowly but surely, the horse will find a way to build on the relaxation we have discovered together, and eventually they get to the point where they don't feel the need to defend themselves anymore. At that point, the horse's own internal and external softness can come through as well.

One of the main components here is for us to maintain our self-control to the point where our internal and external softness remains intact regardless of what the horse is offering. If the horse is tight and we are internally quiet and soft, we are creating an opening for them to connect to softness. If the horse is tight and we're internally and externally worried and tight, the only thing available to the horse is worried tightness.

I've heard of trainers and instructors over the years who've told their students "feel" can't be taught. It's not true. Anything humans are capable of doing, humans are capable of teaching. In fact, "feel" is factory-installed equipment in humans. Without it we wouldn't have survived on this planet as long as we have.

Not only can "feel" with horses be taught and learned, but *all* aspects of feel can be taught and learned, including the internal aspects we've been talking about. Granted, diving that deep into skill development isn't for everybody, nor does it need to be. But for those who choose to venture down the path, I can say with some certainty the revelations you'll find along the way will make the trip well worth it.

CONSIDERING THE HORSE —THIRTY YEARS LATER

CHAPTER 13

Looking Back, Looking Forward

"One day, in retrospect, the days of struggle will seem the most beautiful."

SIGMUND FREUD

I t's been thirty years since I wrote *Considering the Horse,* and in the immortal words of The Grateful Dead, what a long, strange trip it's been. Only a few short years after the book was released, I'd gone from scraping out a living training horses, to being hired on as livery manager at one ranch, then ranch foreman on another.

While still foreman on the ranch where I fully expected to work until I eventually retired, the owners suddenly decided to sell out. The new owners were fundamentalist Christians who, after a year with me as their foreman, decided to let me go because (as they put it) I wasn't a "good enough Christian" to be working on their ranch.

The week after being let go, I called a woman I'd coincidentally met at the ranch during the last week I was employed there. She had encouraged me to go out into the world and do horse-training clinics full time. She told me she'd be happy to be my business manager, which would entail setting up the clinics, and all I'd need to do is show up and do them.

At the end of that phone call, she told me she'd check with a few of her contacts and get back with me. A couple days later, I had a month-long clinic tour booked in Australia, a three-week tour booked in Europe and the United Kingdom, and several more clinics booked in the United States.

My original plan was to use the clinics as a stop-gap measure to bring in some income while I looked for another ranching job somewhere. As things turned out, no ranching jobs were available, but more and more clinics were. In fact, there was actually a time when the harder I searched for a position on a ranch, the quicker clinic bookings came in.

One of the reasons I wanted to get away from clinics and back into ranching was because I felt chronically awkward doing clinics. I was much more at home when things were just me and the horse out on some smallholding somewhere, trying to work things out together. Without a lot of formal horse training education, much of my experience had been gleaned through trial and error where the stakes for success or failure weren't all that high. If I tried something with a horse and it worked, great. If I tried something and it didn't work, that was okay, too. There was seldom anybody looking over my shoulder, telling me I was right or wrong or I should do things this way or that, and there was never anybody comparing what I was doing with how someone else would do it.

That all changed when I started doing clinics, especially in the United States. Back then, there were already a whole raft of established clinicians making the rounds, many of whom were promoting one-size-fits-all training programs with catchy phrases and gimmicks and who had legions of loyal followers. I was the new kid on the block who traveled with a canvas bag (inside of which were two pairs of cotton driving lines, a web halter or two, three or four halter ropes) along with a saddle and pad, all piled in the back of my pickup. Truthfully, I think the only thing that brought people to my clinics in the first place was the fact I already had two books out and a third on the way. I was the next new thing to come around, and I think folks wanted to see what I was all about.

For the first year or two, I'd say over half the questions I fielded from auditors and riders alike began with, *Why don't you do that like so and so?* Many more comments I received fell into the, *That will never work,* and *You can't do it that way,* category.

Here's an example of the kind of things I saw and heard back then. On the first day of a clinic, a woman brought in a mammoth donkey she was having trouble getting to stop under saddle. We spent the first session helping the donkey figure out how to give to pressure from the bit, ultimately teaching him how to stop and back up.

When the woman and donkey came in on the second day, I recapped for the auditors what we'd done in the previous session. We then began covering the things we'd helped the donkey with the day before, including backing up, which he did softer than the previous day.

While the donkey was quietly moving backward on request from his rider, a woman in the audience who had not been there the day before, stood up and loudly proclaimed trying to teach donkeys to back up was a waste of time because donkeys are physically incapable of backing up. Again, this was while the donkey was already backing.

At any rate, with few ranching opportunities available to me, I continued muddling my way through clinics, eventually finding a comfortable rhythm based on things I believed to be true and correct with horses and people. Slowly but surely, the riders and auditors who weren't all that interested in what I had to offer dropped away and were replaced by those who were.

Interestingly, it was about this same time where the popularity of the one-size-fits-all horse training programs began to slip a little. Many of these programs were designed around skewed interpretations of horse herd dynamics in which the claim was the horse that pushes other horses around in the herd is the "boss" or "alpha" horse. To that end, a good deal of what the programs taught was that horses needed to see their owners as the alpha of the herd. As the alpha, the owner then had permission to use however much pressure was needed to get the horse to respond to even simple requests. These kinds of arbitrary outbursts on the owner's part usually only succeed in causing the horse to feel unsafe, and as a result, a fair few horses had more than a little trouble getting on board with the idea. Not surprisingly, problems ensued.

This was all taking place in the early days of what was, and still is, referred to as the "natural horsemanship" movement. The overall marketing theme behind the movement was *if it's "natural," it's got to be good.* Unfortunately, there is very little we can do with horses that is truly natural for either us or the horse, and there wasn't anything natural about the programs being offered, either.

What these programs did was foster an atmosphere of doing things *to* the horse to achieve a goal, rather than doing things *with* the horse in order to develop a relationship. This was the case even though many of the programs touted relationship as the primary focus.

About this same time we also began seeing an influx of one-size-fits-all expatriates. These were well-meaning folks who went into one of the "horsemanship programs" expecting to develop harmony with their horses, only to come out a year or two or three later with horses they could barely get along with. Many of these horses had been on the receiving end of so much mindless repetition during their training and handling, they were either almost completely shut down or so defensive they didn't want to have anything to do with anybody.

This was a bit of a turning point for me. Most of these horses had already been "techniqued" half to death, and because of that, we quickly found using more technique to try to help them feel better certainly wasn't going to be the way to go. These horses helped me understand there are times when it's best to step away from technique altogether and instead lean a little more on blending with what's in front of you, then offering a little direction when the opportunity presents itself.

I didn't know it at the time, but this way of working with horses and people would eventually become one of the core principles of what we do to this day.

———

In amongst all of this, I was also running into certain equine professionals who caused me to rethink long-held notions I'd had regarding other aspects of horsemanship. This began with running into a saddlemaker who built his saddles on trees that were biomechanically sound in relation to the horse's back. After getting to know this maker and studying how his trees fit horses' backs, I could easily see how proper saddle fit could help eliminate a good deal of potential problem behavior in horses.

I eventually bought a good working saddle for Buck from this maker, which he wore until he passed, and which I still have. I also bought a saddle from the maker to travel with so when I ran into a horse with a poor-fitting saddle, I could switch saddles out and see what, if any, changes there were in the horse's behavior. If the saddle made a positive difference, I would put the rider in touch with the maker.

At a clinic in Tennessee, a fellow came in with a sorrel Quarter Horse that, while doing everything his owner asked, always seemed just a little jumpy. It was clear the saddle he was using didn't fit the horse very well, and I suggested trying our spare saddle to see if it made a difference.

After the rider got off, I double-checked the fit of his saddle, which was very tight over the horse's withers and scapula, as well as on his lower back. The saddle also *bridged*, creating about an inch-and-a-half gap between the bars of the saddle and the top of the horse's back just about where the rider sat. It was one of the worst-fitting saddles I'd seen to that point and was sure the other saddle, while probably not a perfect fit, would no doubt fit a whole lot better than this one.

We switched out the saddles and as expected, the new saddle fit much better. We were even able to improve the fit a little more by using a couple small shims just behind the horse's scapula. Once we did that, he had plenty of room over his withers and scapula, plenty of relief over his lower back, and no sign at all of bridging.

Happy with the way the saddle fit, the rider got on and almost immediately the gelding went into a bucking fit. The rider stayed with him and got him stopped, but the horse was not happy. The rider gently urged him forward and with the first step, the horse broke in half again.

"I don't think he likes this saddle," the rider said after getting him stopped the second time.

"I don't either," I agreed.

We switched back to the ill-fitting saddle, and the gelding settled right down, even going a little better than he had before we switched saddles.

I guess it just goes to show, even with our infinite wisdom about all things horse, and even when we get it right, the horse still might have a little something to say about it.

Out of the couple hundred horses for which we've adjusted saddle fit over the years, this guy was the only one we found who preferred the bad fit to a better fit. It's funny but even now, over twenty years later, anytime I talk to someone about saddle fit, that gelding always comes to mind. He reminds me that help is only help when the one receiving it sees it that way. Kind of like the boy that helps the old lady across the street only to find she didn't want to get across in the first place.

Along this path of mine, I'd also run into and learned from farriers and trimmers, nutritionists, dentists, bodyworkers, holistic vets, chiropractors, bit makers, and of course, my friend and equine neuroscientist Dr. Peters. All these folks, and more, have helped move my education forward by answering questions I may have had, and generating other questions I didn't even know existed. It serves to prove the point that the more you know, the more you realize you don't know.

For some folks a thought like that may seem daunting, but I don't see it that way. I look back over the past thirty years and see how much better educated the horse industry is in general and horse people are in particular. Of course, having the internet with all the world's information right handy helps, but the internet alone isn't the only reason. Horse people are more knowledgeable today because they make the effort to be more knowledgeable.

When I first came into the industry, it seemed some trainers could and would say or do almost anything to horses and their owners and get away with it. People often took what they were seeing and hearing at face value because they felt the trainer knew more about horses than they did. Those days are all but gone now, and so are a lot of those trainers.

Evidence-based data is so easily attainable today that it takes almost no effort at all to debunk information that even up to a few years ago was taken as gospel. One case in point is the idea that a horse can sense fear in humans, which, in turn, causes worry in the horse.

A study at the University of Guelph in Ontario, Canada, back in 2014 confirmed horses seem to be able to sense fear in humans, but they don't become worried over it. In fact, the study showed horses responded to the human with what we might refer to as sympathy.

In the study, both horses and humans wore heart monitors, then people who were fearful around horses were blindfolded and put in round pens with them. While the human's heart rate increased during their time with the horse, the horse's heart rate in each case went down during the horse's time with the human. On top of that, the horses would lower their heads and move very slowly around the worried humans. The ultimate result of the study was researchers found being in the presence of worried or stressed humans *did not* cause fear or stress in the horses.

Along these same lines, research shows us one of the main reasons horses become worried in any situation is because they don't feel safe. This reminds me of the story I shared earlier about Wayne and his horse Marty and how the folks at Wayne's barn kept telling him his horse was worried all the time even when he didn't look worried (p. 98). Horses aren't like people who can easily hide their worry. If horses are worried, they're worried because they don't feel safe. When they don't feel safe, they won't be able to act like they do feel safe, unless they're emotionally shut down, also known as *learned helplessness*.

I've seen plenty of horses over the years that come into the arena on the first day of a clinic looking and acting pretty troubled, but on the second day they come in quiet and ready to work. A big reason for this is that horses will almost always be more worried in a new place on the first day, because, as we've discussed, they have a *false-positive bias*. Anything out of their comfort zone is a potential threat. Because of that they'll naturally feel better the second day after it has been proven to them the arena is actually a safe place.

Many is the time I've told a rider whose horse struggled on the first day of a clinic that the horse would be better the next day, and the horse almost always is. This isn't because I'm some kind of equine mind reader or that the training we did had some earth-shattering positive effect on the horse. It's because the horse now feels safe. Simple as that.

———

When I first began doing clinics, I used to ride everybody's horses for them, especially if the horse was struggling with a rider. I would get on, get the horse to a good place, and then give the horse back. Over time, I began noticing almost any time I'd see that horse and rider again, the same issue would've returned.

It finally dawned on me what was happening. Because I was riding their horses for them, owners weren't developing the skills needed to resolve the issues by themselves.

Almost without fail, they'd get the horse home, things would be fine for a month or two or three, then slowly but surely, old habits and behaviors would creep back in to the point where they'd almost end up right back where they started.

Three or maybe four years into my time doing clinics, I decided to stop riding students' horses. It was a tough transition for me for a couple reasons. The first was I had trouble watching riders and horses struggle as they were learning how to get along (which was why I was riding their horses in the first place). The second was students doing their own riding forced me to become a better instructor. I had to learn how to describe things that up till then I had only felt, including the feel through the reins.

More times than not, teaching feel through the reins entailed me taking one end of the reins while I was on the ground, while the student took the other from the saddle. Then, together we'd use varying amounts of pressure to get a feel for each other. We'd start with me being the "rider" and the rider being the "horse." Then we'd switch roles.

Primarily what we were doing, among many other things, was introducing the rider to the concept of *pressure without pulling*, which I introduced back in chapter 8 (p. 115). This simply means once we apply a certain amount of pressure, one on a scale of "0" to "10," for instance, then we don't increase the pressure, regardless of how much pressure the horse puts in our hands in response. In other words, once we're at that "1," our hands become stable so if the horse leans on the "1," they will increase pressure on themselves.

My earlier explanation involved tying a rope to a post and then pulling on the rope. If we think of the post as a rider's hands and the person pulling on the rope as a horse pushing on the bit, we can see the harder the person pulls on the rope, the more pressure will be felt because the post isn't moving. Yet, if that person does something as subtle as just "think" about moving the hands toward the post (even without actually doing it) the person will feel an immediate, albeit very small, release. As I said earlier, we have much more life in us than a post does, so our hands will never be perfectly stable, but the idea is the same.

Almost across the board, once the rider played the horse and felt the kind of pressure and release we're talking about, each one would comment on how subtle things between us would get. Then the rider would go off with the horse and, by replicating that same kind of feel, things would usually get better between them pretty quickly.

Simply giving riders the tools to *feel* what they were looking for turned out to be the incentive for them to develop long-lasting skills they may have missed had I just ridden their horses for them. It was about this time when it dawned on me that my job wasn't so much to just help the horse feel better, although that was certainly a big part of it. Rather, my job was to empower riders by helping them improve themselves.

This idea eventually led to the development of the *aibado* courses we teach in which the primary focus, as I mentioned earlier, is helping riders develop internal and external softness, connection, grounding, balance, and power. The fascinating part of these classes is how we've seen student after student come to an *aibado* class in the morning, then immediately be able to apply what was learned when riding the horse in the afternoon.

Today, the vast majority of what we do during clinics is help riders make small, sometimes even unseen, adjustments in themselves, which, in turn, usually creates quite substantial positive changes in the horse. While we do offer riding and handling techniques when necessary, those times generally make up only a small portion of a rider's time with us. Instead, we're almost always able to tweak whatever technique the rider is already using just enough to get the change the rider is looking for.

With all this being said, we've also found the way we approach developing the horse-rider relationship isn't for everybody, and there's certainly nothing wrong with that. Sometimes people have relied on their techniques and mechanics for so long, almost anything other than what they know not only seems a bridge too far, but also a path too far just to get to the bridge.

There have been times when what we have to offer just doesn't resonate with folks, other times when *I* might not resonate with them. Some folks just want their horses to be better without them having to do the work, and some folks literally don't have time to do the work. The bottom line is there are lots of ways to work with horses in a kinder, more thoughtful way, and whichever one works for individuals is the way they should go.

About five years ago, I was presenting at a large horse expo in Ohio and during a slow time one afternoon, Crissi and I were sitting in our booth watching folks file by in the aisle in front of us.

"Things are changing in the horse world," she said, out of the blue.

"What do you mean?"

"The way people ask questions is different." Somebody passing by waved. She waved back. "Anytime people asked a question about their horses in the past, it always began with, *How do I get my horse to...?* At this expo, almost everybody's questions have begun with, *How can I get better for my horse?*"

"Yeah?"

"Yeah." She smiled. "It's nice."

She was right, of course. As she almost always is. Things are changing. People are becoming more aware, more educated, and more empathetic toward horses. Not everybody of course, but enough to start making a difference.

The spark I see carrying this difference into the future is the enthusiasm showing up in the younger generations of horsemen and women as they begin to seek out kinder, more thoughtful, and more effective ways of being with horses. I see this light in the eyes of individuals like our student instructors, eight extremely talented equestrians from all over the United States and United Kingdom. While they all come from different backgrounds and disciplines, each one, in their own way, has chosen to seek out and share with their own students the principles of a mindful existence with horses. Those principles are in good hands.

As for me, thirty years on from writing *Considering the Horse,* I simply could not have imagined back then the incredible ride on which I was about to embark. Every horse in that book had a share in bringing me to that point. Then they handed me off to a whole herd of horses thundering their way into an unknown future, and I was just along for the ride.

Those horses have now taken me literally all over the world. Because of them, I've been to places I never would have been, seen things I never would have seen, done things I never would have done, and met people I never would have met. They introduced me to friends all over the world, and they introduced me to my wife.

Truly, everything I have and everything I am, I owe to horses, and that's a debt I will never be able to repay.

But it won't stop me from trying.

A Visit from Walter

On a Wednesday night in September of 2021, Crissi and I went out to dinner with our friends John and Bernadette Spillane, owners of Happy Dog Ranch in Littleton, Colorado, where we hold our ten-day intensive clinics. We'd gone to one of our favorite restaurants, an Asian bistro not far from the ranch. It was a nice evening, so we decided to take a table in the outdoor seating area situated in a large courtyard.

It was a slow night at the bistro, and we were the only ones seated outside. I had recently finished the second chapter of this book, and after we ordered and before the food came, John and Bernadette asked what was in the chapter. I was happy to share the gist of what I'd written, not only because it was fresh in my mind, but also because it had special meaning to me. It's the chapter where I discuss a number of mannerisms I unknowingly picked up from Walter during my time working with him.

After I described what the chapter was about, I began telling them how Walter would light a cigarette almost anytime he was asked a question, and before answering.

I explained how this always created a thoughtful pause in the discussion, and how I, perhaps subconsciously, had also developed the habit of pausing whenever I'm asked a question.

As I was talking about Walter, something a bit unusual began to happen. The distinct odor of cigarette smoke slowly overtook the table.

"Do you smell that?" Crissi asked. "Is that cigarette smoke?"

The courtyard where we were sitting was between two buildings—the bistro, and another structure some twenty-five or thirty feet away. Behind Crissi and me, the courtyard was wide open and stretched some fifty or so yards to the west. Behind John and Bernadette, who were sitting across from us, the courtyard was also wide open and stretched another thirty or so yards to the east where it ended at a small road. Beyond the small road was a massive parking lot, and beyond that a six-lane main road.

Crissi sat up in her chair and scanned the entire area in all directions.

"Where is that coming from?" she asked, surprise in her voice. "We're the only ones here." The rest of us looked around as well, and sure enough, there were no other people anywhere in sight, not even in the parking lot across the road.

I should point out here that the cigarette odor was fairly strong. Strong enough, in fact, that it seemed we should have been able to see wisps of the smoke. There weren't any. The smell caused us to pause the conversation while we all looked around, trying to find the source, but no source was to be had.

A smile crossed Crissi's face. "I think Walter's here," she said. "He heard you talking about him."

After a minute or two, and while the odor persistently hung over the table, I slowly continued with my story. A few minutes after that, and as I closed in on the end of the story about Walter and his propensity to light up when asked a question, the odor slowly drifted away.

In all the years we've been going to the bistro, nothing like that had ever happened before, and nothing like it has happened since. Not surprisingly, the topic of discussion as we drove back to the ranch after dinner was about the uniqueness of the experience. What made the situation even more unique was how the story I was telling centered around the pause that would occur by Walter lighting up, and how us noticing the smell of the smoke at the table naturally created a pause in the telling of the story itself.

I'm not usually one to jump to conclusions regarding things like this. After all, there could have been some perfectly reasonable explanation for the odor that we just weren't aware of. That being said, by the time we pulled into the ranch driveway, I was feeling pretty comfortable with the idea that Walter had, indeed, stopped by for a visit. After all, what could it hurt?

The ten-day clinic at Happy Dog in September of 2021 was maxed out with twelve participants. Days at these clinics are full and varied. We spend three half-days per week in the ranch's *dojo* working on *aibado* as well as five half-days working cattle, two the first week, three the next. The rest of the time is filled with everybody working on various aspects of horsemanship with either the horses they brought, or with horses supplied by the ranch. We also have two group meetings per day, one before we go out to ride, one at the end of the day. Our morning meetings are designed to check in with everybody, find out what they plan to do with their horses that day, and answer any questions. The afternoon meetings are once again designed to check in, find out how everybody did throughout the day and answer questions.

There is typically a minimum of three instructors at our ten-day clinics. Crissi, our senior student instructor Gray Graves, and myself. Sometimes, some of our other student instructors come in and teach as well, often bringing our instructor numbers up to five or six.

At the time this particular ten-day clinic began, we had a total of seven student instructors in the world. The number of our instructors is low because we look for very specific qualities in horsemen and women before we invite them into that role. Having extensive hands-on horse experience is, of course, a must, but being good with people as well as being a talented instructor is also a prerequisite, not to mention possessing a firm grasp of the overall principles we endeavor to pass along.

There are no specific courses people can take to become one of our student instructors. Rather, we make our choices from people who regularly attend our clinics and whose growth in all the areas I mentioned, as well as several others, reaches a point where we feel the best way for them to progress further is for them to teach what they are learning. We also must feel confident enough in them to trust they will pass along information to students in a kind, thoughtful, and meaningful way.

On occasion, we will have worked with people long enough to know they possess all the qualities we look for in a student instructor, with the exception that we have not actually watched them teach. On those occasions, we will let them know we're considering them for a position, but we would need to see them teach before offering a formal invitation.

One such potential student instructor was at this ten-day clinic. Her name was Jessica. Jessica had been attending clinics for several years and earlier that summer, at another ten-day clinic she attended as a participant, it became clear to Crissi, Gray, and me she would make a great student instructor candidate. The only thing missing was we had not had the opportunity to watch her teach, even though she'd been an instructor at her own farm for years.

Jessica struggled a bit during the first week of this ten-day, not because she wasn't a talented instructor, but because it seemed her nerves were getting in her way. We offered encouragement and a few suggestions on adjustments she could make, and by the end of the first week her natural talent, ability, and skill began to shine.

At the end of the day on Monday of the second week, Crissi, Gray, and I met. After a brief discussion it was clear we all felt she had the teaching skills we look for in a student instructor, and it was time to make a formal invitation for her to join us in that role. This was something all three of us would do together after our clinic day was over, but due to Gray's after-work schedule, she wouldn't be available until Wednesday of that week.

So, two days later, on Wednesday, and immediately following the afternoon group meeting, we got together with Jessica and offered her the position. She graciously accepted. We sat around for the next hour or so discussing the position in more detail, answering her questions, and just visiting in general. As we were finishing up, we invited her and Gray to dinner with Bernadette, John, Crissi, and myself. Gray had a prior commitment and Jessica said she would love to go but wanted to call her husband and a few friends to share her news instead.

That ended up being the night Walter apparently visited us at the bistro.

The next morning during our group meeting, we announced to everyone that Jessica had officially been promoted to student instructor, which was followed by loud applause and enthusiastic congratulations. As things calmed down, I told the group I had something else I wanted to share with them. I then passed along the story of the cigarette smoke from the night before.

I told the group about the second chapter in this book and how I mention Walter's lighting a cigarette as his way to put a pause in a conversation. I told them how the smell of the smoke the night before came out of nowhere, how it hung over our table while I told the story, and how it only went away after the story was finished.

While I was offering all this to the group, I noticed Jessica's expression changed. She went from a broad smile to a look of concern. She also looked as though she wanted to say something but didn't.

After I finished, Crissi and Bernadette, who was also in the group, added their thoughts, after which I looked over at Jessica.

"Can I tell you something strange?" she said. "All last week I had the smell of cigarette smoke on my hands, and I don't smoke."

She went on to explain almost as soon as she arrived, the smell showed up and nothing she did would get rid of it. At first, she'd thought it was the soap she was using, or the hand lotion or the shampoo. But it wasn't any of that. She'd told her husband about it in a phone call and mentioned it to a few of the clinic participants as well.

"Then on Monday of this week," she added. "It just went away."

"That's interesting," I said. "Monday was the day we decided to offer you the student instructor position."

There was a brief pause.

"You know what I think?" Jessica smiled. "I was really nervous when I got here because I was sure I was in over my head. I bet that smell was Walter's way of telling me I was going to be all right." She looked around the table. "We're all going to be all right."

I couldn't agree more.